ADDINGTON
A History

ADDINGTON
A History

Frank Warren

PHILLIMORE

1984

Published by
PHILLIMORE & CO. LTD.
Shopwyke Hall, Chichester, Sussex

ISBN 0 85033 521 3

Printed and bound in Great Britain by
BILLING & SON LTD
Worcester, England

CONTENTS

LIST OF TEXT ILLUSTRATIONS

Drawings by Frank Warren

This work is dedicated to the memory of the late Mr. W. H. Mills who spent many years gathering information about the long history of the Parish and Village of Addington, Surrey.

ACKNOWLEDGEMENTS

Thanks are due to the Croydon Natural History and Scientific Society, and in particular, to Lilian Thornhill and Roy Smith, members of the Archaeological and Local History Sections of the Society.

Acknowledgements are also made to the clergy of St Mary's Church for their interest and encouragement, and to Mrs. Olga Kennedy and Mr. and Mrs. Scott, who have lived in the Village for many years; and whose memories have proved to be both interesting and useful.

Also to Mr. Graham King, whose photograph of St Mary's Church is on the dust jacket.

ACKNOWLEDGEMENTS

Chapter One

IN THE BEGINNING

EVIDENCE OF THE EARLY PRESENCE of mankind in the Addington area is provided by a variety of relics dating from the Paleolithic, Neolithic, Iron and Bronze Ages, which were all found within the boundaries of this ancient parish. Ground on either side of Shirley Church Road, now occupied by the Addington Golf Club, was once known as Addington Common, and a reference to the existence of 25 tumuli or ancient burial mounds was included in a book on land tenures written in 1679.[1] Pieces of urn or crock were said to have been found in one of them, and to have been shown to the historian, Nathaniel Salmon, author of a work called *A History of the Antiquities of Surrey,* published in 1736. It is generally believed that most of them were destroyed in 1914 when the golf course was laid out, but in 1916 a sighting of two of them was reported to the Croydon Natural History and Scientific Society.[2] One was situated on 'Kitchen Hill' which overlooked the site of an old manor house that stood about half-a-mile to the east of the present Addington Palace. The Bronze Age relics were found when the golf course was made, and these, together with other material from the same period discovered on the Monks Orchard estate in 1855, are now in the British Museum.[3]

Mr. Mills, speaking in 1916, referred to 'worked flints' being 'in abundance at Driv Lane'—now known as Bridle Way—leading eastward towards West Wickham from the top of Spout Hill. Similar discoveries were made on the Ballards and Heathfield estates and more flint implements were gathered in the fields south of the Village Road where the ancient skills of flint knapping were practised well into the 19th century.

The authors of *Neolithic Man in North East Surrey*[4] have written of an ancient track which they claim to have traced by way of Cardinal's Gap, near White Hill, Caterham, over Tillingdown and Riddlesdown to Selsdon. At the latter place they thought that the track turned towards Croydon, there joining Ermyn Street. W. H. Mills, however, was of the opinion that a 'spur' branched from that trackway at Selsdon, descending the hill to Addington through Lady Grove Wood —now incorporated in the new housing development known as Forestdale—to cross Featherbed Lane just south of Addington Well and Pumping Station. It would here have joined another track bordered by a row of yew trees. Some indications of such a track still exist at the spot mentioned, on ground now laid out as part of Addington Court golf course. If the spur mentioned by Mills had continued eastward into Kent, it would have crossed a road laid down by the Romans along the eastern edge of Addington. A section of this road still exists as part of Layhams Road, which runs from Addington Road, near Wickham church, south and west round New Addington and Fairchilds, to connect eventually with the main road from Sanderstead to Botley Hill.

Four principal roads were built about the year 80 A.D. by the Roman general, Agricola, and it is perhaps just possible that this ancient road, reaching from Newhaven to the Thames, may have been one of them. Julius Caesar raided Britain in 55 B.C. and almost 90 years later a full-scale invasion was mounted by the legions of Rome. As the Romans marched north and west from their bridgeheads on the south coast, defence positions would have been built along the several routes taken by the invaders. It is possible that the ancient earthworks at Keston in Kent, and Caesar's Well, close by, may have marked the path of some of these forces as they moved into Surrey, establishing another such site at Caterham. A column of Roman troops might have pushed from Kent across the county border at Addington, and established a resting-place for their men on the high ground of Addington Common, as suggested by W. H. Mills in a speech to the Croydon History Society in 1916.[5] He stated that a circular camp of the period had stood within the boundaries of the old Manor Park of Addington near the junction of Shirley Church Road and Spout Hill. The area between Shirley Church Road and the highway to West Wickham was anciently known as 'Coldharbour', a term often associated with the movement of Roman soldiers across the hills and fields of England. Areas known as 'Warbank' exist in both Addington and Caterham, and these, with the Roman roads, the Coldharbours and the encampments, may perhaps be accepted as credible evidence that the influence of the Roman presence was felt, in some measure at least, in this particular corner of the County of Surrey.

Although it is interesting, indeed important, that notice should be taken of the presence of man in prehistoric times, it is to the years between 500 A.D. and the coming of the Normans that we must look for the origins of modern Addington. The internecine warfare of the early Saxon kings did little to enable their subjects to develop their small parcels of land in peace, and many a struggling community suffered as a result. Addington, if tradition is to be believed, was one of the places often overrun in the battles between the rulers of Wessex, Surrey, and the men of Kent. One such occasion of conflict occurred in the year 568 A.D. when Cutha and Ceawlin, kings of Wessex, won Surrey from the king of Kent.[6] The encounter was at Wibbandune, which, we are invited to believe, was the ancient name of the place we know as Wimbledon. The defeated forces of Æthelberht were pushed back into their own county together with their leaders. One direct route from the battlefield to their homes would have led them across the open commons of north-east Surrey, and the last of these spaces would have been the hills of Addington. The possibility that some of

Aethelberht's beaten warriors might have fought and died and been buried on Addington Common will no doubt seem to support those historians and archaeologists who have asserted that the tumuli mentioned on a previous page were of Saxon rather than of the Neolithic or earlier periods.[7]

The early years of the 7th century saw the promulgation of the 'Laws of Aethelberht', king of Kent. These tell us something about the social order of those times. Although the existence of a class of nobles is made evident, it seems that the real basis of Kentish society was the 'freeman', a peasant landholder, independent of any man except the king himself. In Wessex, at about the end of the same century, Ina, king of that territory, also issued laws, revealing conditions somewhat similar to those in Kent. There *was* an aristocratic influence in society, but the peasant landholder was obliged to serve in the national militia and to contribute to a communal fund or tax levied in support of the king.

About the same time as Aethelberht of Kent and Ina of Wessex were making their laws for a secular England, the church authorities were busy rearranging their own organisations. They began a campaign aimed at persuading the land-owning lords to build and endow churches on their estates, for the better administration of ecclesiastical affairs. Wherever such efforts succeeded there was a tendency for churches to be built close to the residences of the landowners concerned. As a result the church's spheres of influence often became concomitant with those of the local lords and the estates of the latter became parishes as well as manors. Thus the separate authorities of crown and church were unified, and the powers of each augmented. In the parishes adjacent to Addington, e.g., Wickham, Farleigh, Sanderstead, and Croydon, this pattern is readily apparent, and their seems to be no reason to suppose that such a link between the manor and the church would have been absent in the case of Addington.

The boundaries of this ancient parish formed a somewhat irregular triangle, illogically balanced upon its apex. To set the extremities of this quasi-geometrical figure in a modern context, the tip of its northern angle was within half-a-mile of Eden Park railway station. Travelling along the shortest of its sides we should reach the south-western corner where Croham Road and Croham Valley Road are joined together. Here the parish boundary turns south-east to reach the highest point of New Addington, near the Fairchilds school. The third side runs along the border between Surrey and Kent back to the Eden Park area. Within this perimeter over 3,000 acres of land were enclosed, those to the north of the road to Wickham being mainly common and heath. There was also a large stretch of woodland. South of the road, Spring Park Wood extended to Kent Gate, where the village road crosses from Surrey into Kent. Open common also covered much of the modern Spring Park area, joining the Shirley and Addington Commons and merging into the Addington Hills and the bare heights of Ballards.

The height of the ground above the Ordnance Datum varies from 175 feet in the north to over 500 feet in the south, the road through the village rising from about 230 feet at Kent Gate to 400 feet in the west, where Selsdon and

Addington meet. John Aubrey, writing in the 17th century, recorded that 'the soil of Addington is gravelly in the north, chalky in the south'.[8]

The administrative centre of both lay and ecclesiastical authority in the area was the village of Addington, which still stands astride the village road, in a valley between Addington Hills to the north-west and the main ridge of the North Downs to the south and east. At the beginning of the 11th century the pattern of Anglo-Saxon society had become almost feudal in character. Land, mostly in large holdings, was held 'of the King' by those close to his person, and/or by men whose loyalty to his cause was considered to be absolute. Around such estates were areas of wasteland serving as divisions between them. These were known as 'meacrs' and belonged to all. It is from that shared ownership that our modern word 'common' is derived. In these areas, woodland and heath, water and marshland, hilly, stony, or exposed territories were usually to be found.

When the Normans conquered England and introduced their own particular brand of feudalism into the country, they found that the system operated by the subjugated Anglo-Saxons had many features in common with their own. Under the earlier regime the local overlords held their lands directly from the crown. The Normans reorganised these Saxon units into much larger holdings, shared between the more important personages among Duke William's followers. In some cases, however, smaller units continued to be held directly from the king. Addington was one such area. The price exacted from each overlord in return for the power and authority given to him included an obligation to serve the king in peace or in war. He had to provide from his own retinue, a given number of fighting men—under his own leadership—whenever called upon to do so in defence of the king's person or of the authority of the crown. It was also usual for a contribution to be made to the king's exchequer, either in cash or in kind. In addition to the above a more personal service was often demanded. This could be to serve as personal champion to the king, or to carry his banner into battle. In some cases the service entailed some kind of domestic, rather than military, duty, e.g., to wait upon his majesty at table as carver, server, butler, or taster. Other men did other things, serving as valet, chamberlain, chaplain, or cook.

Within the jurisdiction of these 'tenants-in-chief' further divisions of land were made. The several holders of these smaller units became 'lords of the manor', giving service in some way to their own 'overlord', and sub-dividing their own lands among 'vassal tenants'. Such tenants paid for their holdings by rendering service to those above him. Payment was made by working on the lord's lands at seed time and harvest, probably paying rent in addition, for the land and for pasture rights. Those holding more than 30 to 40 acres would retain some degree of freedom within the manorial area.

The next group of tenants, in descending order of precedence, would hold smaller parcels of land, and work on the lord's lands for set periods, perhaps two days in every week and three days during harvest. Extra duties would be done between Candlemas and Easter. Ploughing obligations usually included three acres a year as requested, and another three acres as rent for the holding. Lords of the manor helped to start such holdings, all the property reverting to the lord on the death of the tenant. A similar condition applied to the territory held by the local lord 'of the king'. The titles 'villeins', 'bordars', and 'cottars' were applied to people who only held a few acres, between one and five acres apiece, and the land was held only during 'the lord's pleasure'. It has been stated that a 'villein' was not permitted to own property, either in land or goods. More, he was wholly subservient to his lord, and risked punishment—or even death—if he left the manorial territory without permission. If a 'villein' was not actually a slave, a 'serf', the lowest-ranking servant in the set-up, certainly was. He was bound to the land for life, performing the most menial tasks in return for food and a roof over his head.

The holding of a manor in feudal England in the 11th century should not be likened to the ownership of a modern landed estate. A manorial lord was endowed with an authority over his tenants that was almost absolute. His manor courts dispensed communal justice between himself and those who held land under him. Quarrels between tenants, personal or connected with their holdings, were dealt with by the lord of the manor, and his verdict was final. It is very probable that such a situation existed in Addington when William of Normandy sent his inquisitors to survey the lands of England, and to record their findings in the record that has become known as Domesday Book.

Chapter Two

THE DOMESDAY SURVEY

ENTRIES IN THIS FAMOUS RECORD relevant to the north-eastern corner of the County of Surrey show the existence of two separate manors in the area. These parcels of land were then known as 'Eddintone' and 'Edintone' respectively. After the completion of the Domesday Book the spelling gradually changed. By the end of the 12th century it was seen as 'Aedintona', changing a few years later to 'Adingeton'. It appeared in that form at frequent intervals over the next 100 years. Sometime between 1323 and 1330 the variants 'Adynton' and 'Adyngton' were used in post-mortem inquisitions. By the year 1504 the spelling had settled into 'Addyngton', and by the time of James I the modern form of 'Addington' had become established in general use.

All this is interesting enough, yet it leaves the question of the origin of the names entered in the record of 1086 unresolved. At the present time there are two places in England called Eddington, one near Hungerford in Berkshire, the other now part of Herne Bay in Kent. Edingtons are to be found in other counties, two in Northumberland, and one in Wiltshire. The name Addington appears seven times among the place-names of England. A Great and a Little Addington exist in Northamptonshire. There is an Addington in Buckinghamshire, and another in Kent. The fifth Addington is the subject of this history. Two local districts, one near Liskeard in Cornwall, and another near Lunesdale in Lancashire, are also so named. The question is, have all these places, so widely dispersed over the map of England, a common etymological origin?

Major Godsal,[1] writing of the *Conquest of Britain by the Angles,* thought that the endings of place-names could have been a military significance. The invaders heavily defeated a British force at a great battle at Crayford, Kent, in the year 457 A.D. after which the Angles moved from Kent into Surrey. The Major's theory was that names ending in '-ton' were the sites of defensive positions, '-steds' were military outposts (usually on high ground) and the '-hams' indicated pacified areas behind the lines, no longer at risk from attack. On the basis of this theory it is possible that Wickham could have been one of the '-hams', and the '-ton' of Addington might have been the earthwork that was once on Addington Common. A likely site for an outpost would perhaps be found at Sanderstead. Godsal includes Keston and Addington in a list of '-tons' situated between Orpington and Kingston-upon-Thames. In an address by A. F. Major,[2] the speaker conceded that the distribution of '-hams', '-tons', and '-steds' along the North Downs seemed to 'fit in' with the case expounded by the Major, but he added that he had been 'unable to find any military significance attaching to the terms in any of the languages to which they belong'.

A suggestion from Professor Tolley is perhaps even less acceptable. He thought that the 'Edi-' sound came from an Icelandic word 'Edyfall' meaning a 'wild fell', or from 'Ediland'—another Icelandic word—meaning 'desert-land'. Mr. W. H. Mills thought 'that our valley *could* have merited such a term in Anglo-Saxon times'. This was probably a reference to the heather-clad hills and commons along the border with Croydon and possibly also to the high ground on which the first houses at New Addington were built. Some of the early residents dubbed their environment 'Little Siberia' because of its bleak position, exposed to all the winds that blew.

Another idea came from Mr. Thorne who thought that the ending '-ton' meant 'town', and that the place had once been the home of a tribe called 'The Edings'.[3] In *Place-Names of Surrey,* published by the English Place-Name Society, the name 'Addington' is said to have come from an old English personal name 'AEDDA' of which 'ADDA' and 'EDDA' are variants. The same theory was further explained in a letter sent to the President of the Croydon Natural History and Scientific Society in March 1918 by Arthur Bonner, Esq., F.S.A. He stated that in Anglo-Saxon personal names ending in 'a' the genitive or possessive case was formed by the addition of the letter 'n'. Thus the pre-Conquest writing of the name would have been spelt 'Addan-ton', meaning the enclosure or farm of a man called 'ADDA', which could have been spelt 'ADDA' or 'EDDA'. Gradually the 'an' in 'Addan' became 'in' and where this preceded a 't' the 'g' sounded intruded, eventually becoming an integral part of the spelling, hence 'Addington' or 'Eddington'. It is improbable perhaps, that every place called by these names owes its title to an Anglo-Saxon gentleman named Adda or Edda, especially as they are so widely spread across the length and breadth of England. While it has to be remembered that none of the theories so far advanced can be totally ignored, the carefully-explained and erudite theory put forward by Arthur Bonner can probably be accepted as the most likely explanation of the origin of the name Addington.

The entries in the Domesday Record inform us that in the time of Edward the Confessor, the two manors then in this place were in the hands of Osuuard and Godric respectively, two Saxon gentlemen of some standing in the community of pre-Conquest England. Each of the manors was assessed at eight hides. The term 'hide' is of Saxon origin, used in the measurement of land and is generally believed to have meant 'sufficient land to support one family'. The hide, therefore, in terms of modern acreage would have varied in accordance with the fertility of the soil in each particular locality. Fifty acres of good arable soil would, for instance, have been worth a great deal more than a similar area of marshland or barren hillside.

From that simple example it may be easier to understand why there are such widely-differing estimates of the number of acres to the hide, from as few as 30 to as many as a hundred and twenty. When the Normans took over the country they dropped the old Saxon hide and used their own term carucate instead. This was 'as much arable as could be managed by one plough and the beasts belonging thereto in a year, and having meadow, pastures and houses for householders and cattle belonging'. The substitution of the Norman carucate for the Saxon hide would have made little difference to the number of acres in each holding, since both terms referred to the fertility of the soil rather than to the actual space occupied on the ground.

Croydon, too, had been included in the Survey, and had been assessed at 80 hides. At 120 acres to a hide the acreage would have been 9,600, which is fairly close to the total of 9,150 acres quoted as the Croydon parish area when the Inclosure Act of 1801 permitted the fencing of the open lands of Croydon. The amount already enclosed when the Act was passed was 6,200 acres, the remainder including 750 acres of common fields and common meadows, commons, marshes, heaths, and wastes. In addition there were 2,000 acres of 'Commonable Woods, Lands, and Groves'. The assessment made in the 11th century would have had reference to the acreage already enclosed in manorial estates, and the 6,200 acres, divided by 80, would indicate a ratio of 77.5 acres to a hide. A calculation on a similar basis in the area of Addington would result in a ratio of 120 acres to the hide.

The Saxon thegns were followed by Norman lords of the manor. Albert, a clerk, succeeded Osuuard; and Tezelin, the cook, took over Godric's manor. According to the Domesday Book the Osuuard/Albert holding had land for four ploughs, i.e., four carucates. There were also two carucates 'in demesne' and one and a half with 'villeins and cottars'. A similar distribution was recorded in the Godric/Tezelin manor except that the number of carucates with villeins and cottars was two and a half instead of one and a half. If the Domesday figures are added together it will be seen that the two estates held 16 carucates between them, four in demesne, a term meaning 'land attached to the Manor House'.

These figures indicate the amount of soil enclosed within the boundaries of each manor, but no mention is made in the record of any geographical dividing line between them, or of the actual positions of the manorial grounds within the larger area of the parish of Addington. Nor does the record show the extent of the mearc (commons, waste, etc.) relative to either of the manors. The absence of any such information poses some interesting questions: (1) is it possible to draw across the map of Addington, a line which will separate Albert's lands from those of Tezelin?; (2) can such a division give to each landholder a share of the territory in accordance with the ration give in Domesday, i.e., 7½ parts to Albert, and 8½ parts to Tezelin?; (3) can such a division be made to allow for the mearc and show that the acreage of mearc and manors adds up to the total acreage within the boundaries of the parish?

A tithe map of Addington, compiled *c.* 1842, gives a parish area of approximately 3,530 acres, and there is no reason to suppose that any significant variations of that figure have occurred during all the years that passed since the battle of Hastings in 1066 A.D. Within the boundaries of the parish were the areas of the mearc and the two manors mentioned in Domesday, and the acreage of those areas of the parish that could have formed the mearc is shown on the map as about 1,600, probably somewhat less than its extent in the middle years of the 11th century.

The total area of the parish, less the acreage of the mearc, leaves 1,920 acres to be divided between the two manors in the proportions set out in the famous Survey. Albert had 7½ carucates, and Tezelin had 8½, so if the figure is divided by 32, a unit of 60 emerges. Albert would have had 15 of these units, i.e., 900 acres; Tezelin having the remaining 1,020 acres.

The conditions that could be expected to apply to any attempted delineation of the manorial boundaries are likely to have included the following: (1) one of the manors would have included the church; (2) there should be, in each case, some evidence of continuity in the nature of the holding from its earliest days to more recent times; (3) the separate territories should be reasonably self-contained, having demesne and other lands as set out in the Domesday Book.

It is evident to any visitor to the village church of Addington that the building is adjacent to an enclosed area, for some of the old perimeter walls can still be seen, and the entrance to the ancient manorial park is still marked by the lodges and gateway in Spout Hill, Addington. The park is known to have contained the manorial seat since the 16th century, and the present Addington Palace is the last of the manor houses to have been used for that purpose. The foundations of an earlier house are buried beneath the golf course.

On the south-west boundary of the park lies the area we know today as Heathfield. It still retains some of its erstwhile agricultural character, although a large number of houses have been built on the southern part of the territory. The extent of this particular area of farmland was about 250 acres, mainly used for grazing. With the 320 acres of the two farms centred on the village, plus the 450 acres of the old manorial park, we arrive at a total of 1,020 acres, a figure which may, it is suggested, be equated with that part of Addington recorded as being held by Tezelin, and known to him as 'Edintone'.

Of the other manor, that of Albert the Clerk, we know very little. He is recorded in the Survey as holding a manor at Newington in Kent, and another at Windsor, in Berkshire. He was also a chaplain of the court of the Conqueror. It is unfortunate that there seem to be no reliable records from which to learn of his influence upon, or his personal involvement in, the history of Addington. This does not mean that Albert did not live in his manor of Eddintone, at least for some part of his period of tenure. The most suitable site for a messuage

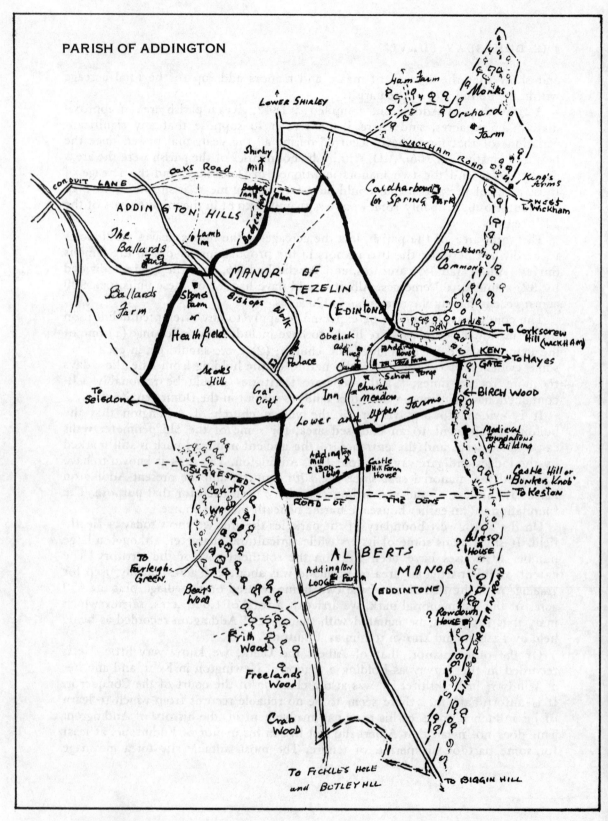

1. The parish of Addington, showing its probable division at the time of the Domesday Survey.

commensurate with the social standing of such a man as Albert has already been allotted to Tezelin, and if that assignment is accepted it follows that the southern heights of Addington must have formed the manor of Albert. It has already been suggested that Albert's share of the territory amounted to about 900 acres, and the combined areas of Addington Lodge Farm and Castle Hill Farm (now the housing complex called New Addington) amount to that figure. A similar acreage is quoted in the will of Sir Olliphe Leigh (c. 1581)[4] in connection with Addington Lodge, which included that particular area. (See Appendix for futher details.)

With the 1,020 acres of Tezelin's property, and the 1,610 acres of the mearc the whole area of Addington parish has been accounted for, and the conditions mentioned above have been fulfilled. A schedule giving the areas and acreages involved is given below, and a map showing where the dividing line between these ancient territories was probably drawn is shown on p. 10. The extent and location of Addington's ancient manors having been estimated, if not fully established, attention must now be given to the individuals who have exercised their authority as lords of the manors of Addington.

Chapter Three

ADDINGTON'S LORDS OF THE MANOR

MORE THAN FORTY INDIVIDUALS have exercised the rights, and enjoyed the privileges, of holding the manorial territories of Addington. The stories of their respective reigns as lords of the manor are told in the following pages, and arranged in chronological order, beginning with the names written in the Domesday Book and ending with the death of the last of the line in 1909.

1. Osuuard, and Albert, the Clerk

That the Saxon thane Osuuard was a man of considerable influence is evident in the number of properties recorded in the Survey of 1086 as being under his control in the pre-Conquest era. We know from that source that he held one of the two manors in this part of Surrey. He also held Totinges (Lower Tooting) and a manor at Godstone. Included in the last-mentioned estate were 15 messuages in Southwark. There were other manors and other estates in the county of Kent, including Harrietsham, Tunstall, and Tonge, Hollingbourne, Norton, and lands in the Isle of Sheppey. He also had interests in Rochester and a small estate near Cobham.

Only one of Osuuard's many manors was allotted to Albert the Clerk in the redistribution of English estates that occurred during the years between 1066 and 1086. That one was Addington, in Surrey. Albert also held lands in Dedworth, Berkshire, and in Upton, Warwickshire. In Rutland he had three churches and two mills. In the last year of his life William I issued two writs transferring the churches to the monks of Westminster. The actual change of ownership occurred after the death of the Conqueror, and the accession of his son, William Rufus.

So far as his manor of Addington was concerned there seems to be no record of Albert's residence in this part of Surrey, even of a fleeting visit to inspect the property he held. Certainly there is no mention of the role he played as lord of the manor, or of any impact he may have made on the villeins and cottars who ploughed his lands, sowed his seed, and reaped his harvests. There is also no evidence that the manor was given to any other officer of the crown—Albert had been a chaplain at William's court—when he died, but as he was a priest, a clerk in holy orders, he would have been a celibate, unable to beget legitimate heirs to

12

his estates. At his death feudal custom would have caused the reversion of his holding to the king. If it is accepted that Albert's Addington territory was situated south of the village road, then transfers of land in that area during the 12th, 13th and 14th centuries would suggest that some fragmentation of the manor occurred soon after his interests in the area had ceased to exist.

In 1241, during the reign of Henry III, part of Albert's manor was given by Walter de Merton to the military Order of the Knights Templar,[1] and in 1249, a parcel of land in Addington was received by the Master of that Order. It was afterwards passed on to the church of St Mary Overie at Southwark. Two fields on Castle Hill, Addington, were once known as 'Temple Fields', and it has been accepted locally that they were once part of the manor of 'Temple', which was later joined to the second of the two manors of Addington mentioned in Domesday.

Sundry other grants of land were made to the London church by individuals holding land in what is now known as New Addington, which are recorded in the 'Addington Charters of St Mary Overie'.[2] There was another manor here on the heights south of the village road. This was held by John de Bures,[3] who sold the property in 1352/1353. The name of Bures was retained in a hill called Buresgate Hill. It was also known as Busgate Hill. This land lay between King Henry's Drive and Gascoigne Road, New Addington, and is now part of Addington Vale, one of Croydon's open spaces.

The de Huntingfield family from Wickham Court, just over the border in the county of Kent, also held land in this part of Addington during the 14th century. All the territories named above became part of one unified manor of Addington in the middle of the 16th century.

2. Godric, and Tezelin, the Cook

Godric, like his fellow Saxon thane Osuuard, held various territories under Edward the Confessor, until the coming of William of Normandy, and the subsequent transfer of lands from Anglo-Saxon to Norman stewardship. Osuuard had held, in addition to his Addington lands, two other estates in Surrey, and some more in Kent. So, too, did Godric, and it is interesting to note that these two thanes who shared the lands of Addington in Surrey should have been close neighbours in Kent as well, particularly in the case of Upper and Lower Delce, parts of the Medway town of Rochester, where their holdings shared a common border. Among Godric's other holdings in Kent was Paddlesworth, on the left bank of the Medway, upstream from Rochester. That manor passed, in the seventh year of the reign of Edward I to Sir Walter de Huntingfield, then the holder of West Wickham, and a member of the family already mentioned as holding part of the Addington manor of Albert the Clerk.

Godric's several estates, however, were eventually taken from him and handed over to followers of William, Duke of Normandy, who by force of arms had become the King of England. The only one of Godric's confiscated territories that need concern us here is his manor of Addington, spelt in those days as 'Edintone', with only one 'd' to distinguish it from Osuuard's 'Eddintone' which had two. In days when we tend to think the spoken word was more easily comprehended than the written version, such a method of identifying the separate manors must surely have confused rather than clarified the situation. The manor went to Tezelin the Cook, or so it is reported in Domesday, but there are no records extant from which we may learn anything about the part he played in the development of his territory in the post-Domesday period. It has, however, been generally accepted that the lands held by Tezelin in 1086 passed from him to a Bartholomew de Chesnaye and were in that person's hands a century later.

3. The Family of de Chesney

The name Chesney—spelt Chesnaye, Chesnet, Cheney, and Caisneto among other variants—is said to have come from Quesnay, a place in Normandy lying between St Lo and Caen.[4] It appeared in England in the Domesday Survey where a Ralf de Caisned is shown as the holder of the manor of Bosham in the county of Sussex.[5] There appears to have been another manor—in the village of Perching—held by Tezelin. It is not unlikely that the manors of Bosham and Perching became united when Bartholomew, an undoubted descendant of the family from Quesnay, acquired the manor of Bosham, together with Tezelin's lands in Perching and, of course, Tezelin's manor of Addington, in Surrey.

How or when de Chesnaye actually came into possession of Addington has never been clearly explained, although a vague reference to a possible marriage between him and an heiress of the Tezelin family has been made.[6] Even then, no date for such a union was suggested. We know from existing records that Bartholomew was in control of the manor in or about 1187, but between that date and the Domesday Record there lies a period of 100 years, about which we know very little. A 'Bartholomew de Chennay' was assessed in Toulouse in 1159 for 'scutage' at two marks.[7] It is suggested that we can relate the de Chennay of this assessment with the de Chesnaye of Addington not only because of the many known variations of spelling that have existed, or that both Quesnay and Toulouse are in France, but also because a similar assessment was made here in Addington. The assessee was a later holder of the manor.

One event took place in the 12th century which is of some significance to the manor of Addington. This was the coronation of Henry II. The 'Testa de Nevill'— a record almost as famous as the Domesday Book—states that Bartholomew de Chesnaye held part of Addington from the king *per serjanciam coquinoe*. That meant that any holder of the manor was required, as a condition of his tenure of the estate, to render some personal service to his overlord, in the case of Addington, to the king. It took the form of presenting a dish—variously described

LEIGH

BARDOLPH

TRECOTHICK

DE CAISNETO (DE CHESNAYE)

AGUILLON

TAIT

LANGLEY

BENSON

SUMNER

HOWLEY

MANNERS-SUTTON

2. The arms of several lords of the manor of Addington.

as 'a white soup', 'dilligrout', and 'gerunt' among other terms—to each new sovereign at his coronation.

There has been speculation as to the ingredients included in this dish which, it is presumed, was fit for a king. One historian has described 'dilligrout' as a 'gruel' flavoured by the aromatic seed of an annual plant called Dill. (Perhaps the word 'scented' would be more appropriate.) In 1794 the Society of Antiquaries published a document entitled 'Royal Household Estate' in which a 14th-century recipe for the dish was given. It apparently included 'Almond milk, Brawn of Capons, Sugar, Spices, Chicken par-boiled and chopped, etc; etc.'. The culinary nature of the offering seems to have encouraged the belief that it originated with Tezelin's acquisition of the manor. After all, the Domesday Record refers to him as 'Cook', and anyone so described should, by reason of his stated profession, be singularly equipped to prepare and present such a dish to a newly-crowned sovereign.

Some doubt is aroused, however, by a work called *The Art of Cookery,* by Dr. William King. In it there is a verse which reads as follows:

> King Hardicanute, midst Danes and Saxon stout,
> Caroused on Nut Brown Ale and dined on Grout,
> Which dish its Pristine Honour still maintains,
> And when each King is Crowned, in Splendour Reigns.

Hardicanute was King of England from 1040 to 1042, and if the verse quoted above is to be believed, it seems to suggest that the serving of a coronation dish of this kind was known in England long before the Normans came. This ties the obligation of 'Magnum Servitum' or 'Grand Sergianty' to the manor itself rather than to the trade or profession of any particular lord of the manor. The fact that such a service was performed by many later holders of the territory of Addington, none of them with any pretensions to the craft of cookery, seems to support such an assumption.

One condition common to an assessment for scutage and to the holding of a feudal manor was the attainment of the age of 21 years. Was Bartholomew de Chesnaye able, having fulfilled that condition, to attend upon Henry II and pledge his allegiance in the manner prescribed?

Some 30 or 40 years after the crowing of Henry, the manor passed from the de Chesnaye family when a husband was found for the daughter of Bartholomew by Richard I. That king reigned from 1189 to 1199, spending much of the period crusading in the Middle East. In order to raise money for these excursions he used many devices, including the selling of honours and properties to those covetous enough and rich enough to pay dearly for them. Some of his funds, however, were gathered from such manorial estates which, by reason of the deaths of their holders had, by feudal custom, reverted to the crown. Among the latter we might have expected to find Addington, and as Richard's need of cash was nothing if not pressing, the early days of his reign formed the most likely period in which de Chesnaye died.

About the year 1185 the 'Church of Edintona' was given by de Chesnaye to the church of St Mary Overie in Southwark,[8] a not unusual gesture made by prominent men of the period when they were nearing the end of their lives. So, by reference to that gift and noting King Richard's interest in the manor, we may make a guess—no more than that—that Bartholomew de Chesnaye died c. 1190-3. In an age when the span of a man's life was rather less than is expected today, 60 would have been near the upper limit of the scale. On the assumption that Bartholomew did reach that age he would have been born c. 1130-3, and attained his majority c. 1154. He would then have been old enough to be subject to scutage, and old enough to have assumed the mantle of lord of the manor of Addington. It is also probable that if he did attend the coronation of Henry II, he was already married.

For his wife to have been a member of Tezelin's family she must have reached her position as 'sole heiress' directly from a male line that had lasted for at least 80 years. She would have had no surviving brothers or nephews, for if there had been any such heirs, one of them would have had the manor, and she would not have carried it as dowry to her husband, Bartholomew de Chesnaye. Such a smooth transition from Tezelin to de Chesnaye must surely be considered as unlikely, especially through the turbulent reign of Stephen, and the equally disturbed reign of his successor, Henry II. Another possibility is that the manor reverted to the crown when Tezelin died, and that Henry II granted the lands to de Chesnaye in the middle of the 12th century. Under such circumstances there would have been no question of a marital link between the two families.

Returning for a moment or two to the Domesday Record, it will be remembered that Tezelin held only one of the two local manors mentioned in that famous survey. The other was held by Albert the Clerk. Because of his ecclesiastical status, confirmed by his holding the office of chaplain to the Conqueror, it would seem reasonable to suppose that his particular part of Addington would have included the local church. We have, however, already noted that the church was given away by de Chesnaye, who had succeeded to the Domesday manor of Tezelin. It is, therefore, clear that the church could not have been in any way part of the territory held by Albert.

When Bartholomew de Chesnaye died there were no male heirs to the manor. His daughter, Isabel, was sole heiress to the estates of her father. It was probably at this point that Richard the Lionheart decided to exercise his right as feudal overlord to escheat the manor. He then arranged a marriage between Isabel and Peter Fitz-Ailwin, who was the son of the first mayor of London. There is no record of any resistance by Fitz-Ailwin to the king's plans for the marriage, and it is to be presumed that the youthfulness, beauty, charm, and social standing of Isabel de Chesnaye were such as to secure his satisfaction with the maiden who 'came with the Manor'.

Peter Fitz-Ailwin came from a family[9] already established in England, probably by the early years of the reign of King Edward the Confessor. An Ailwin Horne, thegn[10] of the king, held the manors of Watton-at-Stone, Walkern, and Sacombe in the county of Hertfordshire. He had three sons, Derman, Aylward, and Leofstan. Derman and Aylward were thegns in their own right. In due course Derman inherited Walkern and Sacombe, and with his brother Aylward, he jointly controlled the manor of Watton-at-Stone. There is a Register of Monasterial Rights[11] which mentions Derman as tenant of Watton, Walkern, and Sacombe.[12] Leofstan, the third of Ailwin's sons, seems to have succeeded to these territories, presumably because his elder brothers had died without issue. He had a grandson, also named Leofstan, who was mentioned in a Charter which had reference to the 'Cnightengeld' and the right of that organisation to certain property.[13] The younger Leofstan had a son, Ailwin, who died in 1165. Henry and Alan, sons of Ailwin, son of Leofstan, paid a fine for lands in Essex and Herts, possibly lands held earlier by their father.[14] Henry Fitz-Ailwin married a lady named Margaret, but her antecedents are unknown. Their London residence was a house adjacent to St Swithin's church, in the City. They had four sons, and these they named in the order in which they were born—Peter, Alan, Thomas, and Richard. Henry Fitz-Ailwin became the first mayor of London, c. 1192-3 and continued to hold that office until his death in 1212. He left some of his lands in London to Richard, the youngest son, and it seems that Alan inherited part of Edmonton. Thomas took over the manor at Watton-at-Stone, and Peter, as eldest son, inherited the rest of his father's property.

It was this Peter who married the daughter of the previous holder of the manor of Addington, Bartholomew de Chesnaye. The marriage probably occurred c. 1190-3, soon after de Chesnaye died, and it is likely that the bride would have been about 16-18 years of age. Isabel Fitz-Ailwin—née de Chesnaye—probably gave birth to her first child, a daughter named Margaret, about a year after the wedding, who is thought to have died before 1215. Margaret married Ralf de Clare, and there were no children of the marriage. Isabel's second child, Joan, was about two years younger than her sister, her birth probably being c. 1196-1198. Since Isabel Fitz-Ailwin is said to have died while Richard I was at the Crusades, her death must have occurred before 1199, in which year Richard himself was dead. Isabel was buried in Bermondsey Abbey,[15] her husband agreeing to pay the monks 15 shillings a year, the amount arising from a house in Addington.[16] (The name of the house and/or its position within the manorial area is not given.) Peter Fitz-Ailwin died before his father, Henry[17] (i.e., before 1212), thus enabling King John of Magna Charta fame to follow his brother Richard's example and arrange that Joan Fitz-Ailwin should marry Ralph Parmentier, merchant tailor, and citizen of the City of London. Ralph confirmed the gift of 11 acres of land in the village of Addington, which Peter Fitz-Ailwin had bequeathed to the Southwark church of St Mary Overie.[18]

The manor of Addington continued to be held by *serjanciam coquinoe*, but the coronation dish was described in somewhat different terms. An extract from that section of the work which has reference to Addington reads, 'Ranulf

Parmentarius held Addington by tenure of "Hastilria". This is the place where "hasta" (the fat of young sows) was kept or provided'.

4. The Family of Aguillon

The 'reign' of Ralph Parmentier as lord of the manor of Addington must have been of short duration, for William Aguillon is recorded to have purchased the marriage of Joan—widow of Ralph—from King John in 1212.[19] As a result of that deal William gained control of the Surrey manor, and of those other manors and estates that had been inherited by his wife from the families of Fitz-Ailwin and de Chesnaye.

L. F. Salzman[20] gives a pedigree that does not include the William Aguillon mentioned above, but suggests that he came from a branch of the family remote from the main branch. Salzman also thought that this particular Aguillon was possibly without any lands held in his own right. If that had been true, it is doubtful if King John would have agreed to 'sell' the young widow and the manor to him at all. John, like his brother Richard, needed gold and cash, and a landless gentleman would be unlikely to have sufficient of either.

The Salzman pedigree, however, does show some possible affinity with the history of the manor in which we are currently interested. There was another William Aguillon—of Salzman's main branch, who had a grand-daughter named Mabel. She married a Gregory de Cheney, who was possibly a scion of the de Cheney/Chesney family who held Bosham and Perching—both in Sussex, where the Aguillons were also landowners of importance, controlling Walton, West-bourne, Nutbourne, and Burpham, either in whole, or in part. Walton and Bosham were adjacent territories. The de Chesneys, as we know, held Addington in the person of Bartholomew, from whom it came to the William Aguillon with whom we are especially concerned.

After William's marriage to Joan Parmentier, and the acquisition of the local manor, he supported the barons who marched to Oxford and told the king that they wanted an end to all his oppressions against them. He was also in attendance when they went to Runnymede to witness the signing of the Magna Charta. When King John died he was succeeded by his eldest son, who became Henry III. The new king was only 10 years old at the time, and Lord Pembroke was appointed to act as Regent. Meanwhile the manor of Addington and the affairs of the people who held it had not proceeded without incident. Even before King John had died, William Aguillon and his wife Joan sued Thomas Fitz-Ailwin (Joan's uncle on her mother's side) for lands in Hertfordshire[21] once held by her father, Peter Fitz-Ailwin. Apparently, King John had called William to him, and the suit was adjourned.[22] In 1217 Joan and William were being sued in their turn. The widow of another of Joan's uncles—Alan Fitz-Ailwin—claimed dowry from some territory in Kent, which Joan had inherited from Alan because there was no issue of his marriage. How these two issues were resolved is not clear, but no doubt some solution was found in due course.

Another question arose in 1220, when William and Joan claimed against Ralf de Clare—who had married Joan's sister, Margaret. The subject under dispute was the village of Greatham in Hampshire, which had descended from Philip de Caisneto to Bartholomew de Chesnaye, and from him to his daughter, Isabel, who was the mother of Joan Aguillon. Ralf de Clare said that two-thirds of the village was held by his mother in dower, and he denied Joan's right to any part of it. Both sides offered to prove their right by 'the body of a freeman' in a duel, but an agreement was reached without a fight, and the freemen were not required to risk their lives after all. Ralf recognised that the land belonged to Joan, in return for which William and Joan paid him 10 marks.[23] William's rights to rents and lands in Emsworth and Warbleton in Hampshire were confirmed by Henry III in 1231. Other members of the Aguillon family held lands a few miles away, at Westbourne in Sussex.[24]

In 1234 Henry III called William to Parliament, and made him a baron. The title was held by tenure and was the only barony of its kind in Surrey.[25] Joan Aguillon died in the same year in which her husband had been honoured by the king, but William continued to carry out his duties to his royal master, and to watch over his own manorial interests. He did have to face a trial of sorts in 1236 when he was summoned to pay scutage. However, he was able to prove to his judges that the scutage roll was wrong, and that he held the manor of Addington by sergeanty.[26] The last-mentioned service, which had been noted in references to previous holders of the manor, was unlikely to have been presented to Henry III for his crowning was a hurried affair. However, Brayley[27] records that William Aguillon held certain lands in Addington by sergeanty of making Hastias in the king's kitchen on his coronation day, or providing someone as deputy to make a dish called 'gerunt', and if suet was used it was called 'malpigernoun'. William Aguillon died in 1244. There is no record of him ever living in Addington, but his involvement in high affairs of state and the extensive estates under his control, must have shed a little reflected glory on this relatively small estate in the north-east corner of Surrey.

Robert Aguillon was the son and heir of William and Joan, and entered into his inheritance on the death of his father. As was the custom in those days he paid homage to his feudal overlord, Henry III, in the sum of £10.[28] Lands from his maternal ancestors included manors in Sussex, Hertfordshire, and in Surrey, and in 1248 he was granted 'free warren' in Perching, Watton-at-Stone, and in Addington. Later, he had licence to crenellate or fortify his manor-house at Perching.[29] Some earthworks of this 'castle' were said to have been visible in the years before the 1939–45 World War.

The right of free warren granted at Perching brought Robert into conflict with John Warenne, Earl of Surrey. The earl claimed that the rights were his because 'his ancestors had lost their lands in Normandy by adhering to King John, and that John had given them free warren in all their lands—for the sake of their name'. The argument was referred to Henry III, who did not accept the earl's submissions. John de Warenne retaliated by raiding the territories held by Aguillon, stationing his men so as to prevent Robert and others from exercising their rights of coursing.[30] In this harassment the earl's men were led by a John de Bohun, of whom more will be said later. In 1253 Robert Aguillon was in Gascony on the king's business when 'certain persons raided his park at Addington and beat his servants'.[31] It has never been established that it was the men of John de Warenne who raided Addington Park, but the actions of the earl in respect of Aguillon's Sussex interests must place him high in any list of likely suspects.

Three years after the local incident Robert Aguillon purchased from Peter de Chauvent the marriage of Joan, widow of John de Bohun,[32] which, in view of the events in Perching and their association with a person bearing the same name, has an air of piquancy about it that is rather interesting. Joan was one of the seven daughters of William de Ferrers, Earl of Derby.[33] Her mother was a daughter of the Earl of Pembroke, who had acted as Regent of England while Henry III was under age, in the years immediately following the signing of Magna Charta. Royal hostility to that document was not removed by the placing of a king's seal upon it, although Pembroke, during the first few years of the Regency, managed to maintain a measure of control over the opponents of the Charta. When Henry III attained his majority, it was quickly seen that he was as much against the Charta as his father had been, and was not really prepared to allow its implementation to proceed smoothly. This led to renewed dissatisfaction, especially from the 25 barons who had sat as a committee of government since the signing at Runnymede. They gathered together several bands of fighting men, and with a citizen force from London, rode off to Lewes in Sussex, where the king was encamped with his army. This was in 1263. The battle that followed should have been won by the king, for his was the superior force, but the barons won the day. Robert Aguillon is said to have been at the battle on the king's side, but if he was, he escaped unhurt, possibly to his house at Addington.

He took part in an expedition against the Welsh, who had rebelled against the king. Aguillon was with the forces besieging Kenilworth Castle where Simon de Montfort had taken refuge. This time the king's men prevailed.

In 1267 Robert was Sheriff of Surrey and Sussex, and at the time of the death of Henry III was one of the King's Council entrusted with the Great Seal of England.[34]

Joan, wife of Robert Aguillon died c. 1266/7,[35] and in the following year the bereaved baron married again.[36] His first marriage had placed him among the members of some of the highest families of the land, and his second venture into matrimony did not in any way weaken his position. The new Lady Aguillon was the widow of Baldwin de Redvers, Earl of Devonshire and the Isle of Wight. She was also the daughter of the Count of Savoy, and aunt of Eleanor, consort of Henry III.[37]

Baron Aguillon's advancement in the social scale was matched by the extensive enlargement of his estates, particularly in the area around Perching in Sussex.[38]

He soon found that his status as a great baron and a large landowner had not improved his relations with John de Warenne, Earl of Surrey, with whom as we have already seen, he had formerly been involved over his 'rights of free warren'. During these encounters Aguillon had fortified his house at Perching, and in 1270, 17 years after the raids on his property in Addington he was licensed, by a similar edict of the king, to 'embattle' his house here in Surrey.[39] The foundations of an old building were found in a wood on the boundary between Surrey and Kent, on the eastern edge of Addington. The discovery was made by Mr. W. H. Mills, in 1916, in the middle of the First World War,[40] and excavations by expert archaeologists could not be arranged at that time. The remains were thought to be medieval, possibly of the latter half of the 13th century, and their relevance to Robert Aguillon's tenure of Addington manor is examined in a later chapter.

Henry III died in 1272 and was succeeded by his son, Edward. At the coronation of the new king, Robert Aguillon, baron, fulfilled his obligation as lord of the manor of this place by presenting his 'yellow dish containing Les Mes de Gyron' at the coronation feast. The name given to this offering seems to have had many variations, but the ingredients, whatever they were, no doubt remained the same as on previous occasions. Robert died on 15 February in the year 1286.[41] His manors and estates included Crofton (Bucks.), Edmonton (Middx.), Greatham (Hants.), Perching (Sussex), and, of course, Addington in Surrey. In addition to the above mentioned, he was patron of the church of St Swythin in Candelwykestrete (Cannon Street), London, and owned other property in the area. In his will he left this London church to the Priory of Tortington in Sussex,[42] and indicated that he wished to be buried there. Margaret, his second wife, lived until 1292, but his heir was Isabel, a daughter by his first wife, Joan. She was 28 years old when her father died, and was married to Sir Hugh Bardolph of Wormegay, Norfolk, and Shelford, Nottinghamshire. The manor of Addington thereby passed from the family of Aguillon to that of the Bardolphs, and remained in their hands for nearly 100 years.

5. The Bardolph Family

Hugh Bardolph, the new lord of the manor of Addington came from a family that had held lands in England for at least a century. There had been an earlier Hugh Bardolph, c. 1187, who had been associated with others in a council left 'in charge of the Kingdom' when Henry II went off to France in 1188. That Hugh died in 1203. In 1243 a William Bardolph, presumably a grandson of the Hugh just mentioned, had livery of his lands, and became lord of Wormegay manor in Norfolk in right of his mother, the daughter and heiress of William de Warenne, a name that has already been seen to have had some influence in the history of Addington in Surrey. William Bardolph was one of the barons appointed by the parliament of Oxford to reform the realm, and was Constable of Nottingham Castle in 1261. He lost that post soon afterwards, but regained it in 1263. He died in December 1289, leaving as his heir the Hugh Bardolph who is the subject of this history.[43]

Hugh Bardolph was born in 1259 and married Isabel, daughter and heiress of Robert Aguillon, c. 1280/81. Hugh became lord of the manor of Addington in 1292 on the death of Aguillon's second wife, Margaret, but he had to wait until 1295 and the death of his own father before he could inherit the manors of Wormegay and Shelford. He was actively engaged with the king's forces in campaigns against the Welsh, the French, and the Scots. His manorial holdings in Norfolk and Nottingham were held under Henry de Lucy, Earl of Lincoln, and with that lord he served at the siege of Caerlaverock Castle. He had previously been present at the battle of Falkirk in 1298. A fellow campaigner at both battle grounds was Sir Peter de Huntingfield of Wickham Court in Kent, a manor sharing a common boundary with Bardolph's manor of Addington, Surrey.

Even before these Scottish excursions Bardolph had been summoned, with other magnates to attend Edward I on 8 June 1294, on 'urgent affairs', and was exempted from a summons to serve the king in Gascony.[44] The *Complete Peerage* calls this summons of 1294 'irregular', and claims that 'it would not serve to create a Barony'. However, another summons dated February, 27, Edward I, was specifically directed to 'Hugoni Bardolf' and it was suggested by the authority quoted that 'Bardolf may thereby be held to have become Lord Bardolf'.

Another reference to a baronial status for Hugh Bardolf was mentioned in a publication made in the early 19th century,[45] where a 'list of such places in Surrey as have been capital residences of Barons by Tenure or writ of summons' includes this entry:

ADDINGTON.   2. Bardolph, Hugh, by Tenure.
Extinct by attainder 6th of Henry IVth.

(The reference to Henry IV is in connection with a later lord of the manor, Lord Thomas Bardolph, who lived in the late 14th and early 15th centuries. His connection with the attainder will be dealt with at a later stage.) The 'Terms of Tenure' applicable to the manor of Addington at the time of Hugh Bardolph were the same as those laid upon earlier lords of the manor, but Hugh had acquired the territory after the crowning of Edward I and was dead before Edward II was king. The ceremonial presentation of Addington's coronation dish did not therefore arise. Hugh and Isabel Bardolph had a son, Thomas, who was born in 1282. When Hugh died in 1304 Thomas was 22 years of age. He did not, however, succeed immediately to the Surrey territories of his father. These had been granted to his mother, Isabel Bardolph, to hold during her lifetime. She was recorded as being of 'Adintone, Surrey' in 1316,[46] and as she came into possession of the manor in 1304, it is possible that she was represented at the coronation of Edward II in 1306 by her son Thomas, who made for the king a dish called 'Mess de Gyron'.

After the death of Hugh Bardolph an Inquisition was held. The enquiry established the fact that 'Hugh Bardolph held, on the day on which he died, the Manor of Addington, Surrey, which was of the inheritance of Isabel his wife, who was the daughter and heir of Robert Aguillon'.[47] It is recorded in the findings of the Inquisition that there was a 'certain capital messuage' in Addington at that time, and that there was a garden adjoining. There is also mention of two parcels of land each containing 120 acres, one worth 5d. per acre, the other having the lower value of 3d. per acre. There were 60 acres in the 'easement Grange' of Waleyngeham (now Warlingham), and they, too, were valued at 3d. per acre. Accommodation for persons attached to the property of the lord of the manor and not being resident in the manor-house, was provided by dwellings standing in the demesne lands around it. These included 25 'free tenements' which yielded an annual rent to the lord of £4 2s. 0d. There were eight 'customary tenants', i.e., copyholders, with annual rents totalling £1 7s. 7½d. Seven cottars paid a total of 8s. 11d. a year for their dwellings. In addition to the rents mentioned, these three groups of tenants had to provide annually two pounds of pepper at 12d. a pound, the copyholders alone finding 55 swine, valued at 1¾d. each.

The Addington residence of the Bardolphs was undoubtedly the building that had been fortified in 1271 by Isabel's father, Robert Aguillon. In the course of strengthening the house against attack the walls would probably have been thickened, and if battlements were added, heightened as well. This work would have extended the life of the building and Aguillon is unlikely to have considered it necessary to build a new dwelling for himself and his family at that particular time, or, indeed, before his death in 1286. When Hugh Bardolph came into possession of the territory he was, as we have already noted, quickly involved in the military excursions of King Edward I. He, too, is unlikely to have embarked upon a new domestic building programme.

There was, however, another building that was featured in the Inquisition Post Mortem of 1304. This was a windmill, valued at 10s. per annum. It must have been among the first wind-driven mills in the country, for it was not until the last quarter of the 13th century that such mills were introduced into England. There were two of them in Surrey, and the one at Addington was still standing in the middle of the 17th century. In Camden's map of Surrey, drawn c. 1610, Addington mill is shown on a hill, and the structure is also indicated in maps of the county until 1659. The second of the two mills stood at Brixton and is also shown on the old maps. The local mill stood in a field still known as Mill Field, opposite the entrance to Headley Drive, one of the modern roads cut across the old farmlands of Addington.

It has already been noted that Lady Isabel Bardolph had a grant of the manor during her lifetime, and she held the territory for a period of 19 years, until her death in May 1323. By an enfeoffment enacted in 1318 the manor passed to her son, Thomas.[48] The influence of the already important Bardolph family had been considerably increased by the acquisition of the manors previously held by the de Chesnayes, the Ailwins, and the Aguillons. These combined territories, scattered from Lincolnshire and Nottingham, through Norfolk, Suffolk, Middlesex, and London, into Surrey, Sussex, and Hampshire, were inherited by Thomas, son and heir of Hugh Bardolph, on the death of his mother, Isabel Bardolph. He had been born on 4 October 1282, at Watton-at-Stone, Hertfordshire, a manor that had once been held by the Ailwin family. It had become part of his inheritance by the marriage of his maternal grandfather to Joan, the widow of Ralph Parmentier.

On 22 May 1306, in the 34th year of the reign of Edward I, Lord Thomas Bardolph was made a Knight of the Order of the Bath.[49] The king died in 1307 and was succeeded by the fourth and only surviving son of his first marriage, to Eleanor of Castile. The new monarch, Edward II, was crowned on 8 July 1307. According to the Reverend D. Lysons' *Environs of London,* pp. 1-6, Thomas served the traditional 'dish' to the king at his coronation and provided two additional portions, one for the archbishop, and one 'for whomsoever the King might choose'. After an active life, spent in the service of his king, a veteran of many conflicts, in this country as well as elsewhere, Thomas, Lord Bardolph died aged 46, in 1328. (The writ for an Inquisition Post Mortem is dated 30 December of that year.) Agnes, his widow, survived him and lived on for almost 30 years, eventually dying in December 1357 at Ruskington, Lincolnshire (*see* the Inquisition Post Mortem for Co. Lincoln, 9 January 1358).[50]

The heir to the manor of Addington, and to all the other lands of Thomas Bardolph, was his son, John, who was born in 1312 and was 16 years of age when his father died. He could not, of course, assume full control of the family fortunes until he came of age. His mother might have managed the estate at Addington as 'trustee' until his 21st birthday, or even have been granted the manor for her lifetime, as had John's grandmother, Isabel, wife of Hugh Bardolph; or the king as feudal overlord could have used his right to escheat the manor, following precedents set by Richard I and King John over 100 years earlier. Edward II, however, was beset with rebellious nobles in Wales and Scotland as well as in England. His wife had taken the heir to the throne to France, where she found a lover—Roger Mortimer. She returned to England with Mortimer and her son, bringing 2,000 French fighting men to take over England. Edward sent an army to oppose the invaders, but it joined them instead. Ultimately he agreed to 'consider' resigning, and retired to Berkeley Castle for that purpose. He was murdered in his sleep by smothering, and his son was crowned King Edward III on 25 January 1327. Under these circumstances it must be considered unlikely that either the murdered king in his last days, or his faithless wife and her lover would have had time to bother themselves with the temporary acquisition of 1,000 acres of Surrey soil. It is here suggested, admittedly without any actual evidence, that from Thomas Bardolph's death in 1328 until his son had livery of his lands in 1335, the manor was administrated on his behalf by his mother, Lady Agnes Bardolph.

In this year 1326, when he was 14 years old, John Bardolph had married Elizabeth D'Amorie who was six years his junior. Her parents were Lord D'Amorie and his wife, Lady Elizabeth, who was the third and youngest daughter of the Earl of Gloucester and Hertford, Gilbert de Clare. Her grand-mother was Joan of Acre, daughter of Edward I. By this marriage with a great-grand-daughter of a king, John Bardolph gained large estates in Dorset to add to the considerable territories that came under his control when he had 'seizen' of his lands on 20 March 1335. John served his king, as his father and grandfather had done before him, in Scotland, Germany, and Brittany. In January 1335 he was called to parliament by Edward III, and he attended as and when required between 1335 and 1 June 1363. In 1345 he was made a Knight Banneret, and he was presumably in France with the king and the Black Prince during the campaigns which included the battle of Crécy, the siege of Calais, and the battle of Poitiers. John, Lord Bardolph, died at Assisi in Italy in July or August 1363. There had been no coronations during his tenure of the manor of Addington, and he had not therefore had the opportunity of presenting to a newly-crowned king the 'Mes de Gyroun or Dish of Dilligrout' in the manner of his predecessors. His wife is reported to have been living in 1360, but the date of her death is uncertain.

William Bardolph, who succeeded to the manor of Addington in 1363/4, hardly merited the appellation of 'lord of the manor' for he was only 14 years of age at the time. In accordance with feudal custom the Crown, in the person of Edward III, granted to Queen Philippa the profits of the property for the rest of her lifetime.[51] Later on, in 1367, the queen placed William, then 17, in ward to Sir Michael Poynings, of Poynings in Sussex.[52] Sir Michael had a daughter named Agnes, and she married young Bardolph, if not actually 'at the Queen's command', then almost certainly with Her Majesty's full approval. The wedding must have taken place before the end of March 1369, for on the 22nd of that month William's wife Agnes gave birth to a son. The boy was baptized and given the name Thomas.

Philippa, Queen of Edward III, died on 15 August 1369, and the 'profits' of Addington manor, which she had been receiving from the previous six years, went to the king instead, and he continued to have the benefit of them during the last year of William's minority. Bardolph became of age on 21 October 1370 and was then able to take full control of all the various estates and manors left to him by his father. He also inherited his father's titles and became William, Lord Bardolph of Wormegay in the county of Norfolk.

The new Lord Bardolph was summoned to parliament by Edward III, and served that king in company with many other peers similarly summoned. He was also called to a parliament by Richard II. The writs of summons were dated 28 December 1375, and 3 September 1385, respectively, and were directed to

'Willeme Bardolph de Wirmegeye' (Wormegay), and confirm that William's title of 'baron' was tied to his Norfolk estate and had no relation to the 'Barony of Tenure' associated with his ancestor, Robert Aguillon, lord of the manor of Addington (c. 1244-1286). William, like other members of his family, fought with King Edward's forces in Ireland and in France.

The coronation of Richard II in 1377 provided an opportunity for William Bardolph to do 'homage' to his sovereign for the manor of Addington, which was held by the service of presenting a dish of 'gerout' to the new king.[53] Although the monarch was only 11 years old at the time, the fulfilment of this ancient feudal obligation no doubt served to confirm Lord Bardolph as lord of the manor of this particular part of Surrey. It is surprising, therefore, to learn that the territory was 'alienated' by Bardolph in 1379 to a William de Walcott for life, with remainder to Bardolph's younger son, also called William.[54] There seems to be no published reason for the transfer of the lands to Walcott at this period, although the clause providing for the reversion of the territory seems to indicate a desire to ensure the future security of young William who in 1379 must have been under 10 years of age.[55] Thomas, his elder brother, had been born in December 1369 and would have been reaching that age himself when the transfer was made. Who William Walcott actually was or where he came from has never been clearly stated, although Manning and Bray in their book *The History and Antiquities of the County of Surrey,* state that 'Dugdale does not mention him, but Blomfield says he was a Knight, and inherited Caistor in Norfolk'. William, Lord Bardolph, died, aged 36, on 29 January 1386. His will, dated 12 September, 9th of Richard 11 (1385), directed that he should be buried in the choir of the church of the Carmelite Friars in Flynn, in the county of Norfolk. His widow had licence—on 10 April 1386—to 'marry whom she would', and she became the wife of Sir Thomas Mortimer shortly afterwards.[56]

Thomas Bardolph, elder son of William, was 17 years of age when his father died. It is to be presumed that he would have had to wait until his 21st birthday before he had livery of his lands, but there is no doubt that he did 'come into his own' in due course of time. Thomas served the king in a Parliament called in September 1390, and attended the king on subsequent occasions as required. In the closing years of the 14th century, however, he became involved with a number of other peers in actions designed to replace Richard II with Henry Bolingbroke, Duke of Hereford. The plotting succeeded, and Henry—a cousin of Richard—became King of England. The early years of Henry's reign were beset with troubles from his erstwhile opponents, and also from the ranks of his own supporters. Among the latter was Richard Scrope, the Archbishop of York; the Earl of Northumberland; and Thomas, Lord Bardolph. All these were in revolt against the king.[57] They were denounced as traitors and their manors and other estates were seized.

The whole issue was resolved in the year 1408, at the battle of Branham Moor, when the king's forces were victorious. The chief leaders of the rebel force were executed, but Bardolph was wounded on the battlefield, and died of his injuries. His body was quartered and the parts sent to four separate cities. His head was exhibited above the gate of the city of Lincoln. Some time afterwards his widow was allowed to have the remains decently buried.

Addington manor, thanks to the action taken by William Bardolph the elder, was not placed under attainder as a result of the defection of Thomas. Its alienation to William Walcott had ended with the death of that gentleman in 1389, and it was returned to William Bardolph the younger. He continued to hold the manor until he died in 1424. There were no direct heirs to the property, and the manor should have descended to the two daughters of Thomas—Ann and Joane. Ann was married to Sir William Clifford, and Joane was the wife of Sir William Phelip. V. Gibbs, Esq., in an editorial note to Cokayne's *Complete Peerage,* p. 460 (d), states that 'by Letters Patent of 19th July 1408 . . . the forfeited lands of Thomas Bardolph were confirmed to Sir William Clefford and his wife Anne, and to Sir William Phelip and Joane, his wife, and to their heirs'.

When William Bardolph died in 1424, it was found that his manor of Addington had been vested in William Uvedale of Titsey. Uvedale came from a family that had been holders of the manor of Titsey for over 100 years, and William himself held the post of Sheriff of the county of Surrey in 1429. A list of 'Knights of the Shire', published in the *Victoria County History (Surrey),* p. 380, includes a Sir William Uvedale (Armiger) as holding that office in 1432 (10, Henry VI) and a William Uvedale who died in 1449 was described as 'of Titsey' in 1434. These separate references seem to indicate that the William Uvedale who held Bardolph's manor of Addington in 1424 was that same William Uvedale who had been Sheriff of Surrey and Knight of the Shire. In the 25th year of the reign of Henry VI (1447) William Uvedale paid the sum of 40 shillings for licence to alienate the Addington territory to John Ownstede, William Bokeland, John Leigh, and others. So the rule of the Aguillons and the Bardolphs, who had held Addington for so many years, was over, and the manor passed into an entirely different family, with no connections whatever with any of their predecessors as lords of the manor of Addington.

6. *The Family of Leigh*

There is some confusion among early historians as to the origins of the Leigh family of Addington. Manning (Vol. II, p. 599) links a John Leigh with High Leigh in Surrey. Hasted, writing about Kent, in his reference to East Wickham in that county, suggests that the Addington branch of the family came from Eastleigh in Kent. Because of this obscurity about the early history of the family, this account is based on a pedigree compiled by Granville Leveson-Gower, Esq., F.S.A.[59] This begins with a Richard atte Legh who appears to have held land in Addington c.1371/2 (45, Edw. III).[60] In 1386 a Richard atte Legh, probably the same person, bought two messuages and 110 acres of land.[61] One of the messuages was in Addington. The other was in Chelsham.

Richard atte Legh is shown in Gower's pedigree as the brother of John atte Legh who was living in 1386 when the land deal was concluded. John was a witness to a Deed, c. 10, Henry IV, concerning Addington.[62] (The date is of interest in that is the year of the battle of Branham Moor, when Thomas, Lord Bardolph put his family's fortunes at risk by rebellious acts against Henry IV.) John's son and heir, as John atte Legh junior, was also a signatory to the same bond. From the marriage of this younger John to a lady whose name is unknown came two children, both boys. The younger of the two, Robert, is said to have had the lease of Addington rectory in 1453,[63] and church records seem to agree, for the list of vicars contains no names of incumbents between 1453 and 1466. The eldest son was named John, and it was this John Leigh to whom the manor of Addington was alienated in 1447.

John Leigh married Matilda, daughter and co-heiress of Thomas Payne of Ockley, Surrey. She died in 1464 and was buried at Addington. John took as his second wife a girl named Alice, said to be the daughter and co-heiress of the holder of 'Botsham' in the county of Kent.[64] The one child of this marriage was named Emma, and she died when she was about 14–15 years old, being buried in Addington church near the north wall of the nave. (The nave was widened at the end of the 19th century, and the original north wall was demolished.) John Leigh held the office of Sheriff of Surrey in 1467, and died on 17 December 1479. He was buried, as directed in his will, 'in the middle of the Church, before the Cross'. There was once a ledger stone set in the church floor, on a spot above his resting-place in the crypt, and on the stone was a memorial brass suitably inscribed. Both stone and brass have been lost for many years, and it is very unlikely that they will ever be seen again.

The marriage of John Leigh and Matilda Payne resulted in the birth of four children, three girls and a boy. One of the daughters married a Walter Waleys of Cudham, in Kent. Another daughter, named Elizabeth, was living in 1512, for she was acting as executrix of the third girl, Joan, who had died, unmarried, on 18 March 1516.[65] The will was signed 'Johan Attlee', and Lysons,[66] and Manning,[67] commenting on the will, attributed it to a 'John Attlee'. Leveson-Gower,[68] however, believed it to be the will of Joan Leigh, sister of Elizabeth, who was her executrix, and of Alice Waleys, née Leigh. There is no record of a John Leigh dying at that time, of or being contemporary with any of the beneficiaries under the will. In that document bequests were made to Nicholas, Anne, and Dorothy, who are referred to as her 'cosyns', although they were, in fact, the children of her brother, John Leigh. She left 12 pence to the 'High Altar' of Addington church, for 'forgotten tithes', and six pence each to the 'Altar of our Lady'; the 'Altar of St Katharine'; and to the 'Altar of Saints Damian and Cosme'. Their names are remembered, together with those of the archbishops who had lived in Addington, on the painted walls of the chancel of the village church.

The only son of the marriage was named John after his father, and succeeded to the property when his father died. In 1486 he was a Justice of the Quorum and Sheriff of the county of Surrey. He married Isabel, daughter of John Harvy of Thurley in Bedfordshire, and sister of Sir George Harvy, whose wife was the daughter of John Chicheley. That gentleman was Chamberlain of the City of London and the nephew of Henry Chicheley, Archbishop of Canterbury. Thus the Leighs were able to claim 'Founder's Kin' with the holder of that high ecclesiastical office.[69]

John Leigh and his wife Isabel had four children. Henry, their second son, settled in Parham, in the county of Sussex. He died without issue, and was buried at Addington. Anne, the eldest daughter, married Thomas Hatteclyff, one of the four Masters of the Household to Henry VIII. The youngest child, Dorothy, married John Wise of Sidenham in Devonshire, as his second wife. Memorial brasses to John Leigh and to Thomas Hatteclyff can be seen in the chancel of Addington church. In the inscription bordering the Leigh brass the date of John Leigh's death is given as 1509. This is wrong: he died on 24 April 1503.[70] The reason for the mistake is not clear, and it is improbable that any explanation will be forthcoming after 400 years. Isabel, widow of John Leigh, had three more husbands and survived them all. When she died in 1544 she asked that her body should lie with that of her first husband, and in accordance with that wish she was buried in the family vault under the chancel of the church.

The heir to the manor of Addington was Nicholas, the eldest of the two sons of John and Isabel, but he was only nine years old when his father died. He could not, therefore, take immediate control of the family estates. His father, however, had appointed Sir Henry Heydon of Wickham Court, Kent, in company with others, to act as trustees of his son's inheritance should his own death occur before Nicholas came of age.[71] This latter event took place in 1516, and Nicholas married Anne, daughter of Sir Richard Carew of Beddington, Surrey. She was the sister of Sir Nicholas Carew, K.G., who became involved in a plot to replace Henry VIII with Henry Pole, Lord Montague. However, the plans failed, and Pole and Carew lost their heads on the executioner's block in 1539. The defection of Nicholas Carew did not apparently affect the fortunes of Nicholas Leigh. The king is said to have visited Addington from time to time, and to have used the Leigh residence as a hunting lodge. Legend has it that there was a subterranean passage connecting the manor houses of Addington and Wickham Court, which was used by his majesty to reach Anne Boleyn when she was staying with her maternal aunt, Lady Heydon, at the Wickham house.

Nicholas Leigh has been reported as being the builder of a mansion which stood immediately above the church and some hundred yards behind it,[72] and the foundations of an old building, on the site indicated, were partially uncovered in 1911. A description of the remains and their relevance to the history of Addington appears in Section Five of the next chapter. By an indenture between Henry VIII and Nicholas Leigh,[73] those parts of Addington previously held by the Knights Grand Cross of the Order of St John of Jerusalem, together with the church, its advowson, and sundry parcels of land which had been held by St Mary Overie church, Southwark, came under the control of Nicholas Leigh. In return Nicholas transferred to the king a number of his other estates. By this arrangement the ancient manors of Addington as recorded in the Domesday Survey were united, and continued in that manner for another 200 years.

The only son of the marriage of Nicholas and Anne Carew was John, who was the sole heir to his father's estates. He married Joan, only daughter and heiress of Sir John Olliphe of East Wickham, Kent, a district now part of Greater London, known as Plumstead. A piece of the old Manor Park still exists in Bostall Woods, and the name of Leigh is seen in Longleigh Lane. When Sir John Olliphe died on 26 June 1577 the manor of East Wickham passed to his grandson, Olliphe Leigh, son of Joan Olliphe, who had married John Leigh, son of Nicholas.[74] John Leigh had died in 1576 and Olliphe Leigh was thus heir apparent to the manor of Addington.

The death of Nicholas Leigh occurred on 30 July 1581, at the age of 86, and he was buried in the village church a week later. In his will he left all his property to 'his well-beloved sonne and grandchild Oliphe Leigh', making Olliphe his 'only and sole executor'.[75] Olliphe's somewhat unusual first name was really his mother's maiden name, used in that way no doubt to ensure the continuity of the family name. The name was used again in this way in the case of two of Olliphe's grandchildren, but seems not to have found favour in later generations of the Leigh family.

When the will of Nicholas Leigh was first prepared and signed, Olliphe was under age, and the testator had included a clause in which he urged his heir 'not to meddle' with his inheritance 'until his age of 21 years'. However, when Nicholas died in 1581, Olliphe was nearing his 22nd birthday and any obligation to heed that cautionary clause no longer existed. Olliphe had married (on 4 July 1577), Jane, the daughter of Thomas Browne, of Betchworth, Surrey. Manning[76] says he was married as *Sir* Olliphe Leigh, but John Leigh, the father of the bridegroom, had been plain 'John Leigh Esq.', and there would have been no hereditary right to the honour or title of knighthood. Brayley[77] records that after the death of John Leigh, 'his son, Sir Olliphe Leigh succeeded'. In either case Olliphe was only 18 years old when he married, and it is extremely unlikely that either Brayley or Manning were correct. Leveson-Gower[78] states that Olliphe became a knight *after* 1586, apparently because he was recorded as 'Olliphe Leigh Esquire' when he donated £10 to a Guildford school. William Camden[79] (writing in 1586), describes Addington as 'the habitation of Sir Olliphe Leigh', and this suggests that the accolade of knighthood was given before that year.

It is said that Olliphe, together with his brother, Charles, had been associated with Sir Walter Raleigh in efforts to establish a British colony in South America. Raleigh returned to England to refit his ship in 1585, and was widely acclaimed for his achievements in the western seas. He was knighted by Elizabeth I, and it is possible that one or two of his associates could have attracted similar awards from England's grateful queen. It is here suggested that the year 1586 is the most likely period in which John Leigh's son became a knight. Elizabeth had kept Raleigh in England after his return, and he stayed here until her death in 1603. James I did not give Sir Walter any chance to renew his seafaring adventures, imprisoning him instead. It is not surprising that schemes for colonising the Americas were laid aside. Charles Leigh, however, was still interested, and with his brother Olliphe's help, set sail for Guiana in May 1604, but things went wrong and Charles died. Meanwhile, Olliphe had fitted out another ship. This second expedition also failed and Olliphe lost a lot of money as a result.[80]

The bestowal of the accolade of knighthood has often been associated with the duties or services rendered to the monarch as a condition of the tenure of feudal manors. It has already been noted that in Addington the obligation laid upon local lords of the manor was a requirement to attend each new sovereign at his coronation, and to present a particular culinary offering. Sir Olliphe Leigh laid his claim to perform that service at the coronation of James I before the Grand Senechal, the Earl of Nottingham, on 24 July 1603.[81] The claim was among many such documents that were marked 'unexamined', placed in a file, and forgotten. It should perhaps have occurred to the claimant that a claim laid only one day before the event with which it was concerned hardly merited any better treatment.

The manorial holdings of Sir Olliphe Leigh were increased in 1593 by the purchase of the manor of Croham at a price of £660.[82] The manor included a 'principal' building described as 'all that tenement or warren house and barn, being sometime a Chapel'. The building stood near the present junction of Manor Way and Croham Manor Road, Croydon. The rising ground behind the site was once called Chapel Hill and the total acreage involved was 229. This included land, wood and pasture, a warren, a 'game of coneys', and the area we know today as Croham Hurst. The association of Croham manor with that of Addington lasted for only eight years. In 1601 Sir Olliphe Leigh sold the territory to Archbishop Whitgift for £740. Part of the estate is now a sports ground under the auspices of The Old Whitgiftian Sports Clubs. A part of the manor containing about six acres and situated in Addington parish was retained by Sir Olliphe and incorporated into his holdings in that parish. Among the other interests of Olliphe Leigh was Eltham, where he held the office of Keeper of the Great Park. When he relinquished the post in 1611, he received £2,227 10s. 0d. in recognition of his sacrifice.[83]

Sir Olliphe died on 14 March 1612, and he was buried at Addington. In his will[84] he left his 'househoulde stuffe at East Wickham, His Coche, Horses and £200 to his wife Jane'. After other bequests he directed that his son and heir, Francis, should, 'within one year of my decease, sett up a monument, whereon shall be sett down the ages, tyme of death, matches and yssues of my grandfather, my father, and myself'. The Leigh memorial in the chancel of the parish church was erected by Sir Francis Leigh in accordance with his father's wishes.

The new lord of the manor of Addington was 21 or 22 years old when he inherited his father's estates. He had married, on 5 June 1610, Elizabeth, daughter of William Mynterne of Thorpe in Surrey. The marriage was a short one, for she died on 2 December 1615, when she was only twenty-two. In the five and a half years between her wedding and her death she had borne four children. There were three boys, named Wolley, Francis, and Olliph, and girl, who was christened Frances. Olliph died in 1623, Francis in 1630, and the second son, Francis, in 1637. Eight years after the death of their mother, Sir Francis Leigh married again. His new bride was named Christian, and she was the daughter of Sir John Thynne of Longleat. Over the next 20 years eight children were born. Three of them died in infancy, but the other five survived their childhood years, all but the youngest marrying and having families of their own.[85]

There seems to be no evidence that Sir Francis ever desired to emulate his father's interest in support of expeditions across the Atlantic Ocean. His local activities, however, aroused some considerable animosity. A Henry Edlin, said to be 'of Addington', had been made to forfeit a sum of £100, pledged as security for a bond entered into by a man named Henry Hayward. Edlin claimed that Sir Francis Leigh had 'violently interfered', preventing Edlin from suing Hayward, who was, according to the claimant, 'well able to pay'. The case came before the barons of the Exchequer in 1631, but Edlin lost the case by default. He failed to attend the Court!

Sir Francis also attracted the displeasure of nearly everyone in the village by closing a highway through Addington manorial park. This had served as a short cut to the road to Croydon which ran round the perimeter of the park. Appeals were made to Sir Francis, but he refused to change his mind. A protest against this decision was sent to the king, James I. Sir Francis claimed that the park was near several of his residences, and that it was 'a place of great delight'. He added that 'the use of the roadway by the villagers disturbed the deer and other game'. The king supported Sir Francis Leigh and notified the Sheriff of Surrey to that effect. There was a condition that another road should be provided outside the park, but whether that satisfied the local inhabitants is uncertain.

Another ancient piece of territory with which Sir Francis was concerned was Croydon Park, stretching from the present railway line at East Croydon over the area now known as Park Hill, and then eastward towards Shirley and the manor of Coombe. Croydon Park was part of the manor of Croydon, at that time in the hands of the archbishops of Canterbury. Francis Leigh held the post of Keeper of the Park for a period during the reign of King Charles I. He had a lodge there, and is said to have lived in the park from time to time. He was Reeve of the Woods, and had all the 'small Spray and rotten trees, grazing for two cows, and a fee of two pence a day'.[86]

In addition to his troubles with the villagers, Francis was also involved in squabbles with the vicar of Addington, James Lesley. It was alleged by the vicar that the lord of the manor had illegally enclosed some land belonging to the church, and that the income of Lesley had thereby been diminished. It was also claimed that Sir Francis had promised to pay the vicar £10 a year as compensation, and that Leigh had not paid certain tithes. Despite support from the archbishop, the vicar lost the day.

In 1625 Sir Francis Leigh had purchased the manor of Bexley to add to his other holdings, perhaps as a residence for some of his children by his second marriage. Several of his grandchildren were baptized there. Grenville Leveson-Gower writes[87] that Sir Francis Leigh was buried at Addington, and quotes an entry in the parish register which gives the date as 17 November 1644. Leigh's will was proved on 19 March 1645.[88] His eldest son by his first wife was Wolley Leigh,[89] who was the presumptive heir to the manors of Addington and Thorpe as well as to sundry other estates. It seems strange, therefore, that Sir Francis should have left his 'Mansion House, woods and Parks in Addington to his son William Leigh'. William was the second son of Francis by his second wife, Christian, and neither William nor his children were in direct line of descent so far as Addington manor was concerned. Sir Francis might have thought that the direct heir, Wolley Leigh, with his obsession with gambling, constituted such a threat to the future prosperity of the manor that it was desirable to make arrangements that would prevent it.

If Wolley had died unmarried and without issue, the local territory might well have gone to his half-brother, William. He did, however, find a wife, in the person of Elizabeth, the daughter of Sir John Hare of Stow Bardolf in Norfolk. There were three children of this marriage: John, who died young; Jane, who married Sir John Lowther, Knight of the Shire for Cumberland; and Thomas, who was his eldest son and his heir. Wolley died on 28 December 1644, only 41 days after his father, Sir Francis Leigh, and young Thomas was next in line of descent. He was only five years old at the time and would have needed someone to act as guardian and trustee. It is probable that his mother carried out these duties, or that William—who had been left the house—took over that responsibility. Whatever happened in 1645, and despite the provisions of Sir Francis Leigh's will, it is certain that at the age of 21, Thomas Leigh presented to Charles II on the day of his coronation the dish of 'dilligrout' which marked the presenter as lord of the manor of Addington in the county of Surrey. It is also written that the newly-crowned king accepted the proffered dish but declined an invitation to taste of the delicacy![90] Thomas was knighted on the same day, and entered into his inheritance.

Some three years earlier Thomas had married, choosing for his bride Elizabeth, daughter and heir of Anthony Rolfe of Tuttington, Norfolk. His youngest son, also named Thomas, died after falling from his horse. It appears that after a party, he left with some of his friends to ride home. His grandmother, in a letter to his elder brother, John Leigh, remarked 'they . . . were then . . . concerned in drink'. The fatal fall caused his sword to break in two, the hilt being forced against his body. This caused internal injuries, from which he died. Wolley Leigh, the second son of Thomas Leigh, was born in 1664, and at the age of 40 he married Mary, daughter of a Mr. Hunt of Hevingham, Norfolk. He died there in 1715. They had one son, Thomas, and two daughters, Mary and Anne, of whom more will be said later. Thomas Leigh, their grandfather, died in 1677. His heir was his eldest son, John Leigh. The new lord of Addington manor had married Catherine, daughter of John Barton, sergeant-at-law, on 28 June 1678. John Leigh attended the coronation of James II in 1685, presented his dish of 'dilligrout' as custom demanded, and was knighted the same day. John was then 25 years old. A son had been born to Sir John and Lady Leigh on 23 February 1681, and was christened John, like his father. Sir John Leigh died sometime between 2 September 1690 (the date of his will) and 17 March 1692, when the will was proved in the P.C.C.[91]

Under the terms of the will Christopher Smith, of Clifford's Inn, London, was appointed guardian of the heir, the 10-year-old son and only child of Sir John and Lady Leigh. Because the testator was anxious that the manors and estates should remain in the Leigh family, even if the present heir died without issue, certain provisions were made. Sir John's will made it clear that if such circumstances did arise, his property should revert to his brother, Wolley Leigh, with the remainder to Sir Francis Leigh of Tring, Hertfordshire. They had a common ancestor in Sir Francis Leigh of Addington, who had married twice. Sir John Leigh was a child of the first marriage, and Sir Francis Leigh of Tring had descended from the other. This will was destined to play an important part in the history of the Leigh family of Addington, a part which will be made clear in due course.

The young John Leigh grew up in the care of his mother and Christopher Smith until he became 21 years old and lord of Addington manor in fact as well as in name. He was present at the coronation of Queen Anne (c. 1702) and, as required by the terms of the tenure of the manor, offered 'dilligrout' to the new monarch. He had married (on 21 March 1699) Elizabeth, the daughter of Sir Stephen Lennard, Bart., of Wickham Court, a mile from Addington, and just over the border between Surrey and Kent. A son was born to John and Elizabeth on 27 July 1702, and was given what seems to have been a favourite name of the Leigh family—Francis. A daughter arrived in May 1704, but she died in April 1705. Two years later, another girl was born, and this time there was a double tragedy, for both mother and child died. They were buried together at Addington on 25 April 1707, the parish register giving the name of the child as 'Dorothy'.

Francis Leigh, son and heir of Sir John Leigh, attained his majority on 27 June 1723. His father's health, both of body and mind, had deteriorated since the death of Lady Leigh to such an extent that Francis decided to assume control of the family estates himself. He continued to do so until his death in 1731.

He was buried in the family vault in the local church. By that time Sir John Leigh was a very sick man, suffering from a progressive mortification of his feet, which needed surgical treatment. His medical advisers were William Vade, an apothecary from Bromley, and a Mr. Douglas, a surgeon from London. Sir John had become |dependent on Vade, not only as his medical attendant, but also as an adviser in the management of his properties. There is no doubt that Vade valued this relationship between himself and his patient. So much so, that he conceived the idea of a marriage between his 18-year-old daughter, Elizabeth, and the ailing knight, who was 52 years old. Vade was also aware that Sir John was the last male representative of the Addington branch of the Leigh family.

On 16 May 1733 the two were married. The ceremony was a private—some might say a secret—affair. The only people present were the principals, with witnesses in the persons of William Vade and Mr. Douglas. The officiating priest was a 'Fleet Parson' who conducted the ceremony in the house of a Mr. Keighton, in Long Lane, London. Despite the unusual venue and the almost clandestine nature of the undertaking, there seems to have been no legal irregularity about this extraordinary marriage, for the couple returned to Addington to live in the manor house, sharing the mansion with William Vade and his wife, and Elizabeth's sister. The event caused much comment among the local inhabitants, for many of them were dependent upon the occupant of the mansion for their very livelihood, and they were naturally worried about their future. However, life in Addington slipped back into its normal pattern, and stayed that way until young Lady Leigh died on 27 January 1736. As there were no children of the marriage it was obvious that if and when Sir John died, changes in the administration of the family estates would be inevitable. Sir John's father had, in his will, said that if his son died without leaving an heir, the properties held by him should go to Wolley Leigh, with the remainder to Sir Francis Leigh of Tring. If that happened, any plans made by William Vade to gain control through the marriage of his daughter to the lord of the manor, might come to nought. However, Sir John lived on for nearly two more years, until 16 November 1737, when he died, between the hours of nine and ten in the evening.

In Addington, as in most of the parishes of the church of England, it was customary for the church bell to be tolled whenever a parishioner died, as soon as the fact of death was known, or as soon afterwards as was practicable. On this occasion the bell stayed silent in the belfry. William Vade had taken Sir John Leigh's will to London where probate was granted to him as the executor named in the will. William Abbott, Seal Keeper of the P.C.C., affixed the court seal to the document on the morning of 17 November 1737. Meanwhile, William Howard, the parish clerk of Addington, had been called to the manor house, where he was given a good breakfast before being ordered to ring the 'passing bell' for Sir John Leigh. This he did, at ten o'clock in the morning of the day after the death of Sir John Leigh.

The timing of the last will of Sir John Leigh is significant. It was drawn up, signed and witnessed, on 30 January 1736, only three days after the death of the testator's wife, and nine days before she was buried in the family vault. By this will, the bulk of the Leigh estates was left to another branch of the family. Addington, with some other properties in Kent and Middlesex, was left to William Vade, and he, as we have seen, was made sole executor.

Immediate steps were taken by the beneficiaries under the will to enter into possession of the properties left to them. The document was disputed by Mary Bennett and Anne Spencer, daughters of Wolley Leigh, deceased, the uncle of the last of the Leigh family to hold Addington. They claimed that they were heirs-at-law by reason of that relationship, and that the will was obtained by William Vade by the exercise of pressure on Sir John Leigh when he was incapacitated by weakness of body and mind. In 1742 the Lord Chancellor decreed that Vade had obtained the settlement by fraud, and that he should return the manor of Addington with the other lands held under the will to Mary and Anne. This was done, but Francis Leigh of Hawley, Kent, one of the others named as inheritors, appealed to the House of Lords. The case was heard before their Lordships on 28 January 1744, and the Chancellor's decision was confirmed. The Addington estates of the late Sir John Leigh remained in the possession of the Bennetts and the Spencers for the next 20 years, by which time the husbands of Mary and Anne were both dead. An Act of Parliament had to be passed in order that the various estates might be divided between the two widows. Addington was allotted to Mrs. Anne Spencer, and in January 1768 she conveyed the manor, with the manor-house, the church and its advowson, and all the lands to Barlow Trecothick, Esq., alderman of the City of London. The price he paid was £38,500. Thus after nearly 300 years in the hands of the Leigh family, a new name was added to the roll of Addington's lords of the manor.

7. The Trecothicks

Barlow Trecothick was born on 30 January 1720 in the parish of Stepney in London, and was the son of a mariner, Captain Mark Trecothick, by his wife, Hannah. Barlow was married 27 years later, his bride being Grizzel Apthorpe, daughter of Charles Apthorpe of Boston, Massachusetts, U.S.A. The wedding was solemnised in that American city on 2 May 1747. Mrs. Trecothick was the sister of the Reverend East Apthorpe who was at that time the vicar of Croydon, Surrey, England. After the purchase of Addington for the not inconsiderable sum already mentioned, Mr. and Mrs. Trecothick entered into their new home, Addington Place. This was the house in which Sir John Leigh had died in 1737. It stood directly behind the village church, about 100 yards from that building, in the old manorial park of Addington.

Barlow Trecothick was a member of the Clothworkers' Guild, one of the ancient institutions of the kind in the City of London. He was made an Alderman of the City in 1764, and held the office of Sheriff in 1766. Two years later he was elected a member of parliament, and continued to hold his seat at Westminster and his seat on the aldermanic benches of the Corporation of the City. The office of Lord Mayor of London fell vacant in June 1770, and the honour of filling that exalted position until the following November was granted to Alderman Barlow Trecothick. He had lost his first wife in 1769, and at some time during 1770 he married again, his second wife being Ann Meredith, the daughter of Amos Meredith of Henbury in Cheshire.

In the year following his second marriage he decided to build a new manor house to replace the one in which he was living, and which had been standing on the site for at least 200 years. His choice of architect fell on Robert Mylne of London, and work began on a new site about half a mile to the west of the existing mansion.[92] Work on the new building started in 1772, and in the following year Trecothick removed the entrance gates and gate pillars from the western side of the old house, and re-erected them on Spout Hill, Addington, where the pillars with the Leigh lions on top of them can still be seen. The lodges on either side were built at the same time to flank a new entrance to his new house, then under construction.

During his comparatively short period as lord of the manor of Addington, Trecothick entered into the life of the community, contributing generously to local activities and paying for extensive repairs to the tower, the nave, and the walls of the church. He died before his new house was ready for occupation, his death occurring on 18 May 1775, when he was 56 years of age. He had obviously hoped for the possible continuance of his name and family in Addington for some time into the future, for he had prepared a burial place under the floor of the chancel. The space had previously held the remains of many of the members of the Leigh family who had died during the long history of their stay in this place. Trecothick removed these remains to the south side of the vault, sealing them in their half of the available space by a brick wall. There is a large stone slab outside the present vestry which covers the entrance to that section of the vault wherein some members of the Trecothick family lie entombed. Unfortunately both of Barlow Trecothick's marriages were childless, and after his death the estate passed to his nephew, James Ivers. James added the name Trecothick to his own, and as James Ivers Trecothick, assumed control of the estate. He married Susannah Margaret Edmonstone, the daughter of Sir Archibald Edmonstone of Duntreath, Stirlingshire, Bart. The new house, called Addington Place like its predecessor, was finished by Barlow's heirs in 1780, and in 1793 the architect, Robert Mylne, provided plans for extensions to the building, and for alterations to the church. The old mansion was demolished some time afterwards.

Whether James ever lived in the new house is not made clear in any records available at the present time, but it is certain that he was still responsible for the manor in the last few years of the 18th century. On 19 July 1797 an Act of Parliament authorising the enclosure of the common lands of Croydon received the royal assent. Some of the lands affected were part of the Addington manor, and James Trecothick, as owner of the manors of Addington Temple, Bardolph and Bures, which extended into Croydon parish, claimed that his rights and interests might be harmed, and he asked to be heard before any irrevocable decisions were made under the Act. As a result, some parts of Addington Hills, and some lands in Croydon on which certain annual payments were due to him, became part of his manor and were incorporated into the parish of Addington.

The interest of the Trecothicks in their territory in this part of Surrey seems to have ended on 22 October 1802 with the signing of a contract between James Trecothick and a Mr. Thomas Coles.[93] By this instrument Coles agreed to buy the manor of Addington. James died at Broadstairs in Kent on 11 September 1843 aged eighty. His remains were brought back to Addington and lie in the family vault beneath the chancel of the village church.

Thomas Coles did not for long enjoy the territory he had acquired. He was, or had been, operating a profitable trading enterprise among the islands of the West Indies, but recurring troubles in Jamaica had ended in the loss of his assets, and he died in 1805, a ruined man. He was succeeded by his son, William Coles, who in 1808 sold the whole of his inheritance to the Archbishopric of Canterbury. The diocese was to hold Addington for the next 90 years.

8. The Archbishopric of Canterbury

The ancient status of Addington as a feudal manor, held 'under the Crown' by an all-powerful local 'lord', was perhaps already declining when Sir John Leigh, last male representative of the Leigh family of Addington, died in 1737. The long legal battle between rival claimants to the estate did nothing to arrest the process in an age which was hearing the first rumblings of the industrial revolution. After the settlement of the Leigh lawsuit the manor was entrusted, as it had been six centuries before, to a merchant of the City of London, in the person of Barlow Trecothick, of whom something has already been said. His early 13th-century counterparts were seen in Fitz-Ailwin, son of London's first mayor, and Parmentier, a Merchant Taylor of the City. Trecothick's nephew, James, who inherited the property from his uncle, made no great contribution to the local community, and left the area in the last years of the 18th century to live in Kent. In the early years of the 19th century the authorities of the Church of England were considering the purchase of a 'summer' residence for the archbishops of Canterbury, and in 1807 or 1808 they acquired Addington Manor, and changed the name of the manor-house from Addington Place to Addington Palace. It is perhaps of interest to note that from 1079 to 1758 51 earlier archbishops have resided from time to time in another ecclesiastical palace in the town of Croydon just three miles and a half from Addington, which old building is still standing, used as a school for young ladies.

The first archbishop to live in the 28-year-old 'new' mansion of Barlow Trecothick was Charles Manners-Sutton, the fourth son of Lord George Manners-Sutton, and the grandson of John, third Duke of Rutland. His rise to the position of 'first subject under the Crown' had been achieved with remarkable speed. Born in 1755, he was a Bachelor of Arts at 22, Master at 25, and at 27, Doctor of Divinity. In 1791 he was Dean of Peterborough, and before his 40th birthday had been appointed Bishop of Norwich and Dean of Windsor. His appointment as Primate of all England was not inconsistent with his previous progress through the lower ranks of the Anglican priesthood. The story of his elevation to the see of Canterbury is interesting. Early in 1805 John Moore, the archbishop, had died. William Pitt, prime minister at that time, wanted Dr. Tomlin, Bishop of Lincoln, to be the next archbishop. The king, George III, had other ideas. He made a special visit to the Dean of Windsor, who was giving a dinner-party to some friends, interrupted the meal, told the host that Moore had died, and appointed Manners-Sutton Archbishop of Canterbury there and then. Thus the king was able to pre-empt Pitt's nomination of Tomlin. In Lord Stanhope's *Life of Pitt* it is recorded that when king and premier next met, '. . . language so strong had but rarely passed between Sovereign and Minister'.

Perhaps it was a sense of gratitude for the favour shown to him that prompted Archbishop Manners-Sutton to erect a stone in commemoration of the beginning of the 50th year of the reign of George III. It was set up on top of a hill in the manorial park at Addington, where it could be seen only by invited guests of the archbishop. It bore words suitably fitted to mark 'this auspicious and happy day' (25 October 1809). The stone is still there, in a secluded spot, in a quiet unbroken except for the sound of club on ball on one or other of the adjacent golf courses.

The archbishop was, of course, at the coronation of George IV in his official capacity. As the lord of Addington manor, he also had to present the dish of 'dilligrout' demanded by ancient feudal custom. On this occasion the 'obscure and delicate dish' was described as a 'herb pudding boiled in a pig's caul'. Was not that 'a dainty dish to set before a king'?

In 1778 he had married Mary, the daughter of Thomas Thoroton of Screveton, Nottinghamshire, by whom he had two sons and 10 daughters. The archbishop was well liked by the local inhabitants of Addington, as a fair and generous lord of the manor. Particularly so by the village boys perhaps, for he threw shillings to them, at least to such of them as doffed their caps to him as he rode past. He had lived at Addington for a part of each year during his term of office, but was at Lambeth Palace when he died on 21 July 1828. He was buried at Addington in a vault specially built under the floor of a small vestry that stood against the north wall of the church. The structure was removed in 1875/6 when the whole building was widened, and the site of the vault is now covered by pews. A memorial tablet can be seen near by.

Dr. Charles Manners-Sutton was succeeded as Archbishop of Canterbury by William Howley, D.D., M.A. He was the only son of William Howley, vicar of

Bishops Sutton, Hants, where he was born on 12 February 1766. After an impressive educational career he became Bishop of London, and was made a member of the Privy Council in October 1813. During his days at his palace at Lambeth he is reputed to have lived 'in considerable state'. As archbishop, and in company with the Lord Chamberlain it fell to his lot to inform the 18-year-old Princess Victoria of the death of her uncle, William IV, and to follow that solemn task at a later date with the more joyful duty of placing the Crown of England upon her youthful head.

William Howley married Mary Frances, daughter of John Belli of Southampton, on 29 August 1805. There were five children of the marriage, two boys and three girls. His eldest son died aged 23, and the younger boy at the early age of six years.

The archbishop played an influential part in the affairs of Addington, greater than that played by his predecessor, and far in excess of his successors. Only two years after his elevation to the see of Canterbury and his coming to Addington, he added a chapel, a library, and other buildings to the existing mansion. With the help of his wife the gardens around the house were greatly extended and improved, earning the praise of J. C. Loudon in his *Encyclopedia of Gardening* in 1829. Brayley[94] tells us that the improvements to the house were designed and executed by the architect Henry Harrison. Brayley also notes that the archbishop was in residence at Addington for six months of every year, and that the extensions to both mansion and gardens gave employment to many villagers.

In 1837 the parishes of Addington and Lambeth were transferred from the diocese of Winchester to that of Canterbury. In 1843 the archbishop financed further repairs to the church. The outer walls were repaired and refaced, and inside the church the walls were cleaned, repaired where necessary, and redecorated throughout. The old pews were replaced with 'backed' seating to accommodate 260 people. A new stone font was installed, not in the tower where the present font now stands, but near by, at the western end of the nave near the pillar of the south aisle. Howley also provided a new porch, the one that is in use today. The letters W.C. that can be seen over the entrance stand for 'William Cantuar'.

The archbishop also contributed to the communal well-being of the parishioners by providing Addington with its first 'piped' water supply. This was drawn from a spring in the woodland above the upper of Trecothick's Lion Lodges on Spout Hill. Pipes were laid to a point in the wall that bounded the park, the water issuing from an 'outlet' or 'spout'. Thus it is said did Spout Hill get its name. Before the water was laid on the name of the hill was Shaw Hill, and it is interesting to note that on a tithe map of Addington of 1842, now in the keeping of Croydon public library, the hill is actually marked Shaw Hill. The water supply was installed in 1844, and in the same year Addington got its first National school. This, too, was mainly due to the great interest shown by the archbishop in local affairs.

According to Edward Walford[95] Howley was a pattern of dignity, meekness, and benevolence. Both Lambeth Palace and Addington Palace were improved

3. Archbishop Howley's water supply in Spout Hill (from a drawing by W. H. Mills)

while he held the primacy. He was greatly liked in Addington and in Shirley. Both parishes shared the administrations of one vicar for a short period. Archbishop Howley died at Lambeth on 11 February 1848 and was buried at Addington. His memorial can be seen in an alcove in the north wall of the chancel near the altar.

John Bird Sumner was enthroned in Canterbury cathedral on 28 April 1848. He was the choice of a 'Whig' prime minister, Lord John Russell. He was born at Kenilworth, the son of the Revd. Robert Sumner on 25 February 1780. He married, on 31 March 1803, Marianne, daughter of George Robertson of Edinburgh, a captain in the navy. In the year 1818 Sumner was offered the living of Mapledurham in Nottinghamshire. He became a prebendary of Durham

4. The village school, Spout Hill; used for over 100 years, it has now been demolished

cathedral in 1820, retaining his canonical status until 1848, when he succeeded William Howley as Archbishop of Canterbury.

Unlike the earlier archbishops who had occupied Addington Palace from time to time, improving and enlarging the property, and taking an active part in the village community, very little is known of his influence on the local scene. He did attend at the House of Lords from time to time, and was once a member of the Poor Law Commission. He died at Addington on 6 September 1862, and was buried in Addington churchyard. The archbishop, two of his daughters, and some other relatives lie in graves in the north-east corner of the churchyard. An iron railing surrounds the plot.

Charles Thomas Longley, successor to Sumner as Archbishop of Canterbury, was born at Boley Hill, Rochester, Kent, on 28 July in the year 1794. His father was Recorder of Rochester and a magistrate of Thames Police Court. Charles Longley had a brilliant educational record, and after a career in holy orders which began in 1822 he became headmaster of Harrow School in 1829. He was the first Bishop of Ripon when that diocese was formed in 1836. He became Bishop of Durham in 1856, and then held the Archbishopric of York until his translation to Canterbury on 30 October 1862.

In the section of this chapter which dealt with Archbishop Manners-Sutton, mention was made of the obelisk he erected to mark the jubilee of George III. A little to the east of the site occupied by the obelisk there was once a seat and a table, set upon a mound,[96] which might have been one of the 25 tumuli said to have been in the manor park of Addington from prehistoric times until the construction of the golf course. They were then swept away, except for one or two of the smaller ones. The relevance of this reference to the period of Longley's stewardship of Addington manor, lies in a visit said to have been made by Emma, Queen of the Sandwich Islands, to Addington Palace. During her stay she was apparently shown the view of Shooter's hill, Woolwich, from the spot mentioned. Although the site is now not readily available to the general public, the same view can still be enjoyed today by members of the golf club. Archbishop Longley died of bronchitis at Addington on 27 October 1868, and he was buried in Addington churchyard not far from the wall of the present village hall.

The next of the archbishops to be connected with Addington was Archibald Campbell Tait. His birthplace was Edinburgh, and he was the ninth child of John Tait of that city. Archibald's ancestors were originally Episcopalians, but became Presbyterians in the 18th century. Although brought up in that faith, Tait resolved to become a minister of the Church of England. He went into residence at Oxford in October at the age of 19 years. After graduating with a B.A. degree in 1833, he was made a Fellow of Balliol College in 1834, and was ordained in 1836. His first experience as a parish priest was gained in the parish of Balden, Oxfordshire. He was headmaster of Rugby School in 1842 and after some years became Dean of Carlisle. Later he was made Bishop of London, and while there was offered the see of Canterbury by the then prime minister, Benjamin Disraeli. He was enthroned in Canterbury Cathedral in February 1869. He lived mainly in Lambeth Palace, making only occasional visits to his residence at Addington, rather than staying in the area for some months at a time. He was, however, interested in the parish and the people of Addington, and was not neglectful of his responsibilities as lord of the manor.

In July 1882, the archbishop left his palace in London, and came to Addington where he died on 1 December. Although it was suggested that his body should rest in Westminster Abbey, he was buried 'simply' in the churchyard of Addington church. His grave is not far from that of his predecessor, Charles Longley, in the western part of the churchyard, a little to the north of the Longley grave. A memorial to Archbishop Tait is to be seen in the window at the western end of the north aisle, and the window in the tower is in memory of his son, Crauford Tait.

Archbishop Tait laid the foundation stone of a new Mission chapel in the hamlet of Addington Hills on 16 August 1873. The building was also used as an infants' school from May 1874. At that time there were flint cottages on either side of what is now colloquially referred to as Sandrock Hill. Its real name is Addington Hill. The Mission house still stands, but is now a private residence. During his association with the church and parish of Addington a programme of major repairs, redecoration and reconstruction of the church was undertaken. The archbishop showed great interest in all these activities, frequently visiting the site to see how the work was progressing.

After Archibald Tait came Archbishop Edward White Benson, the son of a chemical manufacturer, in business in Birmingham. Edward was born there 14 July 1829. Educated at Trinity College, Cambridge, he became a Fellow in 1860, and later Master of Wellington College. He was Bishop of Exeter in 1876, and became Archbishop of Canterbury in 1882. He took a great interest in the matters laid before the House of Lords, and was a constant attender at, and a frequent contributor to, the many debates that exercised the interest of their lordships from time to time. He was highly appreciated in his manor of Addington, and the decorated walls of the chancel, and the reredos behind the altar stand as a memorial to the affection with which he was regarded by the local community. His death was sudden and totally unexpected. While attending a morning prayer service at Hawarden Church he suffered a sudden heart attack and died immediately. He was staying with William Gladstone at the Hawarden home of the statesman, and was sitting in Gladstone's private seat in the church when he collapsed and died. He was buried in Canterbury Cathedral on 16 October 1896, five days after the tragic happening at Hawarden Church.

He was the last of the archbishops to spend any part of his time in Addington. Frederick Temple, who succeeded him as archbishop, ended the close association of Canterbury with Addington when he sold the mansion and its grounds to Frederick Alexander English, a diamond merchant from South Africa. The agreement was concluded on 21 July 1898. The new occupant of the building enlarged the mansion and made further improvements in the grounds. He took an active part in local affairs, giving generous support in many cases. He made an application to the appropriate authorities asking permission to present the ancient offering of 'dilligrout' at the coronation of Edward VII, but the application was refused. His sojourn in this ancient village, however, did not last for very long. On 2 June 1909 Frederick Alexander English died, and with his death the last fragile link with the ancient feudal manors of Addington was broken.

After the demise of Mr. English, the estate was left in the hands of trustees who sold part of the old park to the Addington golf club in 1913. The headquarters of the club are in Shirley Church Road, on the northern edge of the estate. Most of the remaining territory was bought by the Addington Palace golf club, the course being laid out across the park from Gravel Hill to Spout Hill. The course is bounded on its southern side by a recreation ground, which itself lies against Addington Village Road, now renamed Kent Gate Way. Other parts of the original manorial park have since been sold and used for housing development.

Summary

Of the two manors mentioned in the Domesday Survey, that held by Albert the Clerk was apparently divided into at least two sections, which were recognised at a later date as the manors of Temple and Bures respectively. The descent of the other manor, held by Tezelin the Cook in 1086, has been reasonably well documented, and it can be said with confidence that more than 30 individuals have had the right to be called lords of the manor of Addington. They can be divided into family groups as follows:

(a) De Chesnaye, Fitz-Ailwin and Parmentier.
(b) William and Robert Aguillon.
(c) Five members of the Bardolph family.
(d) Eight representatives of the Leigh family.
(e) Barlow and James Trecothick.
(f) Thomas and William Coles.
(g) Seven Archbishops of Canterbury.
(h) F. A. English, Esq.

In addition to the above, Isabel, widow of Hugh Bardolph held the manor for a time. So did William Walcott and William Uvedale at the end of the reign of the Bardolph family. Mary Bennett and Anne Spencer, nieces of the last of the Leighs, shared the responsibility for the Leigh estates for some years, and kings and queens have had a hand in the affairs of the ancient manors of Addington.

Of the families mentioned let us take the first three. They were all inter-related, the manor having passed from one family to another through the female line. The Aguillons and the Bardolphs were involved in the shaping of national events, the former with the drafting and the signing of the Magna Charta, the latter in the early skirmishing which preceded the Wars of the Roses. Representatives of both families had fought in France, in Scotland, and in Wales, and attended parliaments whenever the reigning monarch so commanded.

The Leighs, however, were not so deeply or so personally involved in the intrigues and dangers of the affairs of kings. It is true that the brother-in-law of Nicholas was mixed up in a plot to supplant Henry VIII, and that legend tells of a castle, presumably held by the Leigh family, that was 'razed' to the ground by Cromwellian troops, but apart from these incidents members of the Addington branch of the family seem to have merited and retained the notoriously fragile friendship of successive monarchs. The 14th-century ancestors of the family were probably from yeoman stock, and in acquiring the manor of Addington from Uvedale after the Bardolphs had left, did so with the intention of establishing Addington as a base from which future generations could spread their name across the land. The family connection lasted for nearly 300 years until the death of Sir John Leigh in 1737, which left the manor without a male heir. The continuance of Addington as a feudal manorial holding was on the decline from that moment.

Barlow Trecothick no doubt cherished the wish that his own name might continue to be associated with the territory in the future. His action in moving the remains of the Leighs to one side of the chancel vault in order to make room for members of his own family might be considered to support that view. But the effort was made too late in Trecothick's life, and his successor had interests elsewhere.

Finally there were the archbishops. For the first 50 years of their presence in Addington their interest in the new summer residence was reflected in their concern for local affairs. During the remainder of their stay the periods spent by the archbishops of Addington became less frequent, and at the end of the 19th century Archbishop Frederick Temple sold the house and the lands to F. A. English, Esq. He died in 1909, and the property was split up. The parish of Addington was later absorbed by the town of Croydon and that once independent county borough has been lost in the amorphous anonymity of Greater London.

Chapter Four

ADDINGTON'S ANCIENT MANOR-HOUSES

IT WAS STATED in the previous chapter that the headquarters of Addington manor were in Addington Park. That area is now shared by two golf clubs, some residential properties, and a recreation ground, but the last building to have been used as a manor-house is still standing, occupied by the Royal School of Church Music. We know the house as 'Addington Palace', but when it was built in 1780 it was called 'Addington Place'. It has replaced an earlier mansion that had stood behind the church near the modern houses in Roxton Gardens, a turning off Spout Hill, Addington. The foundations of the old manor-house are still there, under part of the Addington Palace golf course. Some 17 individuals are known to have exercised their manorial authority from one or other of the mansions mentioned above, and it is obvious that their predecessors must also have resided in Addington from time to time, if not within the ancient park, then somewhere in the vicinity of the village and the church.

The earliest known reference to a manorial park in Addington was in 1253,[1] when it was raided during the lord's absence abroad, and the first mention of a house that might have been associated with that park was in 1271.[2] In that year King Henry III gave permission for a 'house at Addington' to be embattled, an act that may account for the legend of a castle in this ancient place. There are several sites on which such an edifice, or any subsequent manor-houses could have stood, and it is the purpose of this chapter to examine each of these positions, and assess their relevance to the history of Addington.

1. Birch Wood

The most interesting indication of a possible medieval site to emerge in modern times was due to Mr. W. H. Mills, a well-known local historian. In 1916, on one of his many excursions within the parish, he went walking in the woods that straddle the eastern boundary, and he found among the trees to the south of the village road, the foundations of an old building. From a drawing made by Mills it can be seen that the walls were of considerable thickness, well able to resist attacks from marauders. The building was basically oblong in plan, as would be expected in a medieval house standing in the 12th century. The overall dimensions of this basic area were 74ft. by 31ft. 6ins. This space would probably

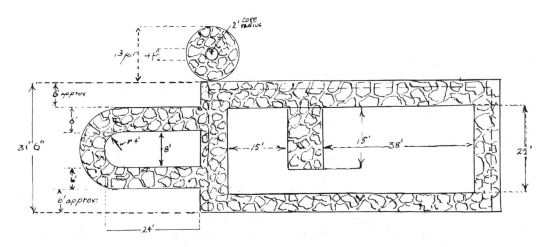

5. Plan of foundations found in Birch Wood in 1916. The building was thought be be medieval, possibly 13th century (from an original by W. H. Mills)

be one large hall, open to the roof timbers 20ft. or more above the floor. The circular shape at the north-east corner shows an outer diameter of 13ft., with a core diameter of 4ft. It seems apparent that a tower once stood upon the spot, possibly containing a spiral stone staircase. The apse-like structure on the north wall could have been part of the original building, but it is possible that it could have been added at a later date. The tower seems to be contiguous to the main structure rather than integral with it, and the 'apse' could also be described in this way. It is also to be noticed that there is a variation of 18ins. in the thickness of the west wall as against comparable measurements in the other walls. If it is assumed that all four walls were of uniform thickness when the building was erected, and that the apse and tower were additions to the fabric. Might not all three be indicative of reconstruction or reinforcement operations resulting from the royal licence granted to Robert Aguillon in 1271?

The wall shown projecting from the east wall seems rather stouter than would be expected in a wall dividing the hall into two sections. If it had continued above floor level it could have contained a chimney, although a more usual position for a medieval fireplace was in the centre of the floor area, smoke escaping through a louvered aperture in the roof. A stairway could have existed within its thickness, but that would deny the suitability of the free-standing tower for gaining access to the battlements authorised by Henry III. If this very heavy wall contained neither hearth nor staircase it might have housed the entrance to the legendary escape route supposed to have run between the manor-houses of Wickham and Addington. The legend is common to both manors and one end of the tunnel is said to still exist somewhere close to

Wickham Court. It would certainly have been easier to have constructed a tunnel between these two points than to carry such a feature beneath the road to an exit point nearer to the village.

The ridge behind the village road to the north continues eastwards until it reaches West Wickham at the top of Corkscrew Hill. Clothing the southern slope of the ridge is Spring Park Wood. It is probably the remains of an ancient forest that stretched from the heights of Norwood and Sydenham through Penge and Beckenham to Addington. That part of the wood that fell within the boundaries of Addington parish was, if we are to believe tradition, often visited by Edward I, who became king of England at about the time when the embattlement of Aguillon's house was completed. The king is reputed to have enjoyed hunting in the manorial hunting grounds of Addington, and if the ancient foundations in Birch Wood are really those of the building fortified 700 years ago, his majesty may well have rested there from time to time.

From the foregoing paragraphs it might be thought that Mr. Mills had discovered the beginnings of a chain of manor-houses that ended in Addington Park where Addington Palace now stands. The foundations are obviously those of a building of considerable importance, with walls of impressive thickness, even in those early security-conscious days. Churches, however, are frequently found with walls of comparable thickness, and ecclesiastical architectural practice, both before and after the Conquest, produced buildings not very dissimilar to the ground plan of the house we have been considering.

Between 1240 and 1311 the religious and military Order of Knights Templar (founded to provide protection for pilgrims to the Holy Land) held land in Addington. We are reminded of their presence by two fields called Upper and Lower Temple Fields. They are now covered with houses, on ground within easy reach of any house that might have stood in Birch Wood. The possible existence of a home in Addington for some of these religious warriors in the intervals between excursions to the Middle East might well have engendered another of the legends pertaining to this corner of Surrey. This tells of a monastery which, so goes the tale, once existed in Addington, and, if the woodland building found by Mills was ecclesiastical rather than lay in the function it performed, the religious label attached to the Templars might seem to provide a tenuous link with the legendary monastic retreat.

Nothing has so far been found of any wall or fence that might have surrounded an enclosed manorial park similar to that which exists at the other end of the village road, but it is nevertheless apparent that this position among the trees on the eastern edge of Addington must stand high in the list of likely sites for one of Addington's earlier manor-houses.

2. Castle Hill

About a quarter of a mile from the site in Birch Wood is Castle Hill, now lost in the vast development of New Addington. Yet from ancient times until the end of the Second World War (1939-1945) it had been a prominent feature on the southern skyline. John Aubrey,[3] in a reference to Addington, wrote of 'the inhabitants' who 'show a Copped Hill where it is said, stood formerly a Castle'. He added, '. . . the name is retained in Castle Hill'. Stories of a castle must have been current in Addington for many years before Aubrey made his perambulation of the county of Surrey 300 years ago, and the inhabitants mentioned by Aubrey would have readily believed that such a building would have stood on a hill-top, especially such a feature as Castle Hill. That was the opinion held by many historians who had written on the subject before Mills made his discovery of the foundations in Birch Wood, and before the development of the area for housing purposes. The woodland remains have been described, and their relevance to the legendary castle evaluated. It would be reasonable to assume that any similar signs of an ancient building on Castle Hill would be found within two or three feet of the surface. Yet when building development began in that area, 15ft. of soil was removed from the top of the hill, and nothing was found of any such building, nor of smaller structures that might have been associated with a manor-house or castle. Although Aubrey has recorded that 'groundsels and other vestigia of ruined buildings' have been turned up from time to time, he gave no details of any such finds, the places where they were found, or of the periods to which they may have belonged.

Nearly every historical record has made reference to Castle Hill, and it seems to have been accepted that all such statements indicate the same spot. This feature is shown on the current Ordnance map as half a mile east of Castle Hill Farm, which had its farmhouse in Lodge Lane, just north of Headly Drive, at its junction with that highway. There has, however, been some confusion in relating the position of the hill to the position of the church. In Edward Walton's *Greater London* (Vol. 2, pp. 130-136) the hill is said to be 'near the Church', and in *The Gentleman's Magazine* (1799) the words 'on an eminence adjoining the Church' appear. In a work entitled *Croydon in the Past,* published by the *Croydon Advertiser* in December 1883, it was described as 'overlooking the Church'. The hill is nearly a mile from the church, too far to be described as near. For the same reason it cannot be considered as 'overlooking' that building. 'Adjoining' presupposes a closeness that is not apparent where Castle Hill is concerned. Canon William Benham,[4] vicar of Addington 1867-1873, once wrote that 'the fortified house of Robert Aguillon was certainly somewhere on Castle Hill', and if the whole terrain, from the county boundary to Lodge Lane is considered to be one single hillside, Benham's somewhat vague indication of the probable site seems the more acceptable of the ideas that have been mentioned above.

One possible position in the larger area of search thus made available was suggested in a news item[5] published in July 1973. This reported a subsidence that had occurred in two roads in New Addington. The roads referred to were Walton Green and Horsley Drive, laid across fields which were once part of

Castle Hill Farm. The place is only marginally below the 400ft. contour line of the Ordnance map, and is part of an escarpment having Castle Hill at its eastern end, and Castle Hill Farm at its western extremity. When flats were being built nearby, workmen came across a tunnel or culvert about 5ft. in diameter. The subsidence, if that it what it was, and the story of the workmen's find, remind us again of the legend—already mentioned in relation to the site in Birch Wood— of a tunnel connecting the manors of Addington and Wickham.

If an archaeological examination of the site in the area of Walton Green and Horsley Drive had been possible it might have confirmed a reference to such a feature contained in a tale told to Mr. W. H. Mills in 1910. Mills had asked an old inhabitant what he knew about a castle standing somewhere in Addington. and his informant—a Mr. Henry Antram—replied, 'Yes, I've heered say there was an old Castle Place used to stand there out in the fields beyond Addington, and I've heered as how some solgers came round by Wallingham[6] and Chelsham way with their guns, and after the head ones had a meeting with them at the Castle up in Parley Field, they couldn't agree, so the solgers bombarded it and levelled it to the ground, but them at the Castle didn't get hurt, as they escaped underground to Wickham Court. This was in old Oliver Cromwell's days . . .'.[7] Among the papers left by Mr. Mills[8] is one with a rough pencil sketch, showing a section of the county boundary. It shows a culvert running across the border by Rowdown Wood, almost opposite Mickleham Way, and only half a mile from the so-called subsidence near Horsley Drive. The possibility that this culvert might have been part of Antram's 'underground passage' to West Wickham cannot be ignored.

The period of Oliver Cromwell's Commonwealth was from 1649 to 1660, and the holders of Addington manor were on the side of the royalists, so an attack from the parliamentarians was always likely to happen. It is interesting to note that a gap occurs in the parish registers from 1653 until 1701, and this could be explained by the upheaval caused by the siege described by Henry Antram. He talked of a field called 'Parley Field' in which a meeting took place. This field is shown on the tithe map of Addington as 'Parlour Field'. The change in spelling and pronunciation can surely be attributed to the normal corruption that occurs over several generations. The field is now covered with houses, the earliest erected in 1927-1928. The ancient boundaries of the field have their modern counterparts in Gascoigne Road—between Heneage and Shaxton Crescents—then along the last-mentioned road to the top of the rise, then left along the ridge to Salcot Crescent. The field was only about 500 yards from the subsidence area. It is also interesting to note that the fields now covered by North Downs Crescent, North Downs Road, and the east side of Parkway were known as 'Comp Fields'. Our interest in them lies in the meaning of the Anglo-Saxon word *comp*. According to Bosworth's *Anglo-Saxon Dictionary*, p. 165, it means 'a battle, a contest, or a camp'. Could the 'solgers' of Antram's tale have waited here with their guns for the result of the parley in 'Parley' or 'Parlour' field?

It seems to have been generally agreed by earlier writers that the house Aguillon was allowed to embattle was pulled down at the end of the 14th century. That was about 250 years before the Cromwellian period, and if there was a Castle Place as Antram said, it could not have been the Aguillon house. There may have been an earlier structure on this site, and a clue may be found in the notes already written about the foundations in Birch Wood. Mention was there made of two fields called Upper and Lower Temple, and it was suggested that these fields could point to the remains in the wood being those of a house belonging to the Order of Knights Templar. Comparisons between maps of the New Addington area and the Addington tithe map show that the Horsley Drive–Walton Green junctions on the modern map actually fell within the boundaries of Upper Temple Field as marked on the tithe map. In fact, this site would seem to have a stronger claim to an association with the Templars than the building that once stood in Birch Wood. It is, therefore, the more unfortunate that an excavation and examination of the site is now impossible.

3. Addington Lodge

Albert's Domesday manor of Eddintone would almost certainly have been divided after his death, which probably explains the fact that in 1317 Sir Walter de Huntingfield of Wickham Court was in possession of part of the Addington Lodge area, i.e., that part of Addington lying south of Castle Hill Avenue. These fields later came into the hands of John de Bures, and he eventually sold his 'manor' to a William de Winkeworth.[9] In 1352 a house known as 'Roughedoune' was sold by de Bures to Sir Richard Gurney. The name is remembered today in Rowdown Wood and Rowdown Crescent. The building was thought by W. H. Mills to have stood between the last-mentioned road and Vulcan Way, New Addington, on what was once called Northey Down. Another ancient dwelling is thought to have stood by the woods at the end of Kestrel Way, New Addington, about 600 yards north of the supposed site of the Roughedoune house. King Henry's Drive crosses a valley between Gascoigne Road and the factory estate area, and the hillside was once known as Buresgate or Busgate Hill. The likelihood of John Bures having lived at either of the sites mentioned is lessened somewhat if reference is made to three maps of the district. These were drawn by John Senex (1729); J. Stockdale (1798); and Shoberl (1808). All of them show a 'capital messuage' where the Croydon Borough Highways Depot is presently situated. The building was known as Addington Lodge Farmhouse for many years, but for the last 50 years it has been called Fisher's Farm. The name of Bures was mentioned in the Croydon Inclosure Awards of 1801[10] in which it features in conjunction with the names of Bardolph and Temple. The farmhouse may even be the site of a manor-house of Albert the Clerk. Should it ever be possible to make an archaeological examination of the site some interesting results may be expected.

6. Addington Lodge Farmhouse, *c.* 1900 (an impression)

4. Church Meadow

In the first section of this chapter reference was made to Baron Robert Aguillon. He was the son of William Aguillon who had acquired the manor 'in right of his wife', the daughter of a previous holder, Bartholomew de Chesnaye. Before his death de Chesnaye had 'given' the church and 12 acres of the land to the church of St Mary Overie, Southwark. It had been accepted for a long time that the area in question was Church Field or Meadow, situated at the village end of Lodge Lane. The field has now been crossed by a road which takes traffic round the village instead of through it. Ridges seen on the surface of the field were described by some 19th-century observers as earthworks[11] and have been recorded as such by an Ordnance Survey. Other authorities have thought that the varying levels of the soil were due to the formation of lynchets, which marked the boundaries of ancient field patterns. On the basis of this latter theory trenches were cut across two of the lynchets. At a depth of between four and five feet, signs of early ploughing practices were found.[12] Two sets of grooves had been made in the soil, one set superimposed on the other at an angle of nearly 90 degrees. This system of ploughing has been thought to date from Roman times, but cross-ploughing in this manner is known to have continued well into the medieval period of English history.

During the digging process many sherds were found, at varying depths below the surface, and dating from early medieval times. The presence of pieces of pottery, tile, slate and other materials does not invalidate the evidence of ancient agricultural activities, supported as it is by the criss-cross marks of medieval or pre-medieval ploughing. Similarly, the fragments of domestic utensils and ancient building materials found in the field cannot be considered as positive proof that the meadow once contained a mansion that could have been the domain of an early lord of the manor. Yet the presence of the sherds, even if that presence was due to the spreading of midden-waste, presupposes that the materials so scattered were from a building or buildings situated at no great distance from the place where they were found.

Whatever the reason for the ridges or 'earthworks' may be, there is no doubt that there is, in the south-west corner of this field, a raised area of land large enough, and level enough, to have held a manor-house of considerable size and importance. Support for the view that the remains of ancient residences may be buried under the turf of Church Meadow comes from a map of Surrey by Rocque (c. 1760) in which two buildings are shown, one apparently in the above-mentioned corner of the field, the other about 50 yards to the north, and nearer to the village road.

During the making of the new road which now by-passes the village, the foundations of some flint walls were cut through. The archaeological section of the Croydon Natural History and Scientific Society was informed, and an examination of the site was made. The walls were in the position indicated by Rocque as the site of the second building, and the excavations that were made enabled a great many sherds to be discovered. These were from every century from the 12th to the 18th, but were generally larger and in a better state of preservation than those which came from the trenches cut across the lynchets. All of these have been examined and evaluated, and are now in the care of the Society.[13] At this stage it is impossible to say with absolute certainty what sort of building stood upon these foundations, although it seems improbable that the remains uncovered can be those of one of the lost manor-houses of Addington. However, the accuracy of Rocque's map has been confirmed by the finding of the foundations, and there is no reason to believe that the other building shown on the map does not exist.

Just to the south of the exposed walls was an area that had been paved with large cobblestones or pebbles. These had been laid on a bed of gravel beneath which was a layer of chalk. The width of the roadway, if that is what it was, measured 30ft. or 6m. The surface was obviously superior to that which might be found on an ordinary cart track leading into an ordinary field. It appeared to run in the general direction of Birch Wood and the foundations found by Mr. Mills, but it could have been a drive or carriage way to either of the buildings shown on Rocque's 18th-century map. It must be remembered, however, that during the war of 1914/18 there was a searchlight mounted in the far corner of this same field, and the roadway may not have any connection with the more ancient history of the area at all. It may just have been put in to serve the men attending the searchlight!

If further evidence is needed to reinforce the testimony of the map, we have the writings of Canon Benham, vicar of Addington 1867-1873, to which we can refer for information.[14] He wrote of William Bardolph—a 14th-century lord of the manor—who 'pulled down Addington Castle and built a manor house opposite the church, where now is Mr. Still's field'. (In Benham's time Mr. Still farmed all the land on the south side of the village road, and Church Field was part of his farm.) Returning to the subject in 1883 Benham mentioned that he was standing in Addington Park, 'a hundred yards above and north of the Church', and continued: 'Looking over the slope beyond, I see, exactly opposite me, the unmistakable signs of another large house. It is a meadow now, but marks of the foundations are quite plain'.[15] Equally plain, it is suggested, is that Mr. Still's field and the meadow are the same as the field in which we are now interested—Church Field.

An unnamed vicar of Farleigh (c. 1909/10)[16] is said to have recorded that he had seens 'signs of a Castle' which stood in a field 'a little below Castle Hill Farm'. Another clergyman—the Revd. J. M. Hobson,[17] wrote in terms almost identical with those of Benham, of the same ridges and foundations. There is little doubt that each of these clerical gentlemen was referring to Church Fields, or that each of them believed that under the surface of the meadow lay the foundations of one, at least, of Addington's ancient mansions. Are they the remains of the Aguillon/Bardolph castle, or of the house said to have been erected to replace it in the early years of the 15th century? According to Brayley's *History of Surrey* (c. 1850) that building was erected 'on the same site as the Castle', but if the latter structure is found to have stood in Birch Wood or on Castle Hill the former could not have stood in Church Field. The Revd. D. Lysons, however, has said that the new manor-house was erected 'at the foot of the hill',[18] and that would seem to point to Church Field as one of several sites that could be so described.

Mention has already been made of the foundations found during the laying of the new road, and in November 1973 some exploratory digging was done in the field close to the village road between Spout Hill and the new houses opposite the churchyard. Some signs of walls were found which seemed to extend under the houses just mentioned. There was also an area paved with stones like the suggested roadway in Lodge Lane. The paving could have been part of a courtyard or a roadway. The finds appeared to be medieval in origin, although no remnants of domestic ware or building materials were found to assist in dating the discoveries.[19]

The distance of the site from the church is about 80 to 100 yards, and something of relevance to the finds just mentioned may be found in another work by that literary cleric, Canon Benham,[20] This time it is a story, set in the year 1460. Benham's hero was a John Leigh who lived in a manor house, on ground 'slightly rising, exactly opposite the Church, about 100 yards away'. The remains recently uncovered were certainly within the distance given, and insofar as they were on the other side of the road could, perhaps, be described as opposite the church.[21] The thickness of the exposed walls was greater than was observed in the remains found in Lodge Lane, and it would seem that the foundations found near Spout

Hill would be better able to support a building as important as a manor-house. The site is also 'at the foot of the Hill'—at least at the foot of Spout Hill—and the ground south of the site could be described as 'slightly rising'. If the house supposedly built in 1401 was erected here it would certainly have been under the direction of William Bardolph, for he held the manor of Addington from 1389 to 1424.

In 1386 a certain Richard Leigh[22] held lands in Addington, as did other members of his family. Any such territory would have been held by them as tenants of the manorial lord, i.e., William Bardolph. The manor-house that took the place of the castle, and the manor-house in Benham's story could therefore be one and the same. The whole of the Aguillon/Bardolph manor was acquired by the Leighs in 1447, and the reigning head of that family could well have been living in the building in 1460. There is the possibility that the house used by the Leighs was not the one just mentioned, but another house in the far corner of Church Field in the position shown on Rocque's map. It is unfortunate that the examination of these potentially interesting sites in this particular field has had to be abandoned, although it is hoped that arrangements for another archaeological 'dig' can be made before any further buildings are erected in the area.

An acceptance that Church Field is the site of a manor-house must necessarily place the meadow firmly in the ancient Domesday manor of Tezelin, which descended from him to Bartholomew de Chesney and from him through the Aguillon and Bardolph families to the Leighs. The field could not, in that case, have been the 12-acre parcel of land given with the church to St Mary Overie in the 12th century. Mr. Mills had something to say about this when he spoke to the Croydon Natural History Society in 1916.[23] He suggested that the 'long held view' that the field was once held by the Southwark church might be incorrect, and put forward his own idea that the 12 acres belonging to the monks were probably west of Lodge Lane. Pursuance of that theory must wait upon opportunities arising in the future.

5. Addington Place

The ancient boundaries of Addington Park are seen today in Shirley Church Road, Shirley Hills Road, Gravel Hill, Kent Gate Way (part), Addington Village Road, and Spout Hill. We know that the area enclosed by these roads has been shown to have had links with the Stone and Bronze Ages, and that from pre-Conquest times to the early years of the present century it must have had close associations with at least one of the holdings recorded in the Domesday Survey of 1086. No trace of the 'Terra Alberti' mentioned in the record has survived into modern times, but we have from the late 12th century onwards a reasonably good account of the other Domesday manor held by Tezelin. From these records we learn that the territory passed from Tezelin to de Chesnaye, and that he gave the church to a London priory. The transfer was made about

1187, not long before the death of the donor. The church must, therefore, have been part of the manor inherited by de Chesnaye, and could not have been included in Albert's territory despite the ecclesiastical nature of his office.

From de Chesnaye the manor came—eventually—to Sir John Leigh, who died in his house in Addington Park on 16 November 1737. The site of the mansion was 100 yards north of the church, and the foundations of the house are still beneath the soil at the eastern end of the Addington Palace golf course. The date of the demolition of the old Addington Place has been given by various authorities as 1780, but it is possible that the house was pulled down over a period of years, for the *Victoria County History (Surrey),* Vol. IV, p. 164, reports that 'some remains of a medieval house are said to have existed in 1799'.

If the last years of the 18th century saw the disappearance of the mansion, the second decade of the 20th century witnessed a revival of interest in the building. Mr. Mills, on whose collection of Addington lore so much of this work is based, saw the foundations of the old house when they were partially uncovered in 1911. A plan of the remains was prepared in 1912 and this showed that the west wall measured about 140ft. from north to south. The length of the south wall was about 180ft. between the east and west walls, but apparently continued eastward for another 50ft. Eight buttresses, somewhat unevenly spaced, are shown against this wall, and their apparently random positioning, plus the absence of similar features on the other walls, could indicate that the wall became progressively unsafe, and needed this form of support. The east wall seems to stop short of the north wall by some 30ft., but it is probably connected to it at some point below the surface. These three walls are recorded on the plan as being built of flint, a form of construction seen in the church, 100 or so yards away. The north wall is interesting in that it is 'out of parallel' with the southern wall. Two sections of wall separate from the rest are shown, one being parallel with the north wall, the other at right angles to it. The north wall itself is described as 'a chalk wall covered with plaster' and that means that the wall is possibly much older than the flint walls. The materials used here in Addington, together with the 'misalignment' mentioned, suggests that an earlier building may have stood upon the site, its northern wall facing five degrees west of true north.

Mr. Mills was able to excavate part of the basement area in the north-eastern part of the building, and has left us two drawings showing part of the cellar area. The west wall of the cellar (see A on plan opposite) was described by Mills as 'definitely medieval', perhaps older than the outside walls of the house. The brick wall (B) is obviously a later addition. The alcove (C) with its rounded arch is typical of Early Norman (Romanesque) architecture (*c.* 1066 to 1189) and might be thought to support the theory of an older building on this site. The second of the drawings depicts the east wall of the cellar area (D) with some window apertures (E) and a doorway (F) leading to the outside of the house. It would seem that the kitchen and service areas were situated on the eastern side of the

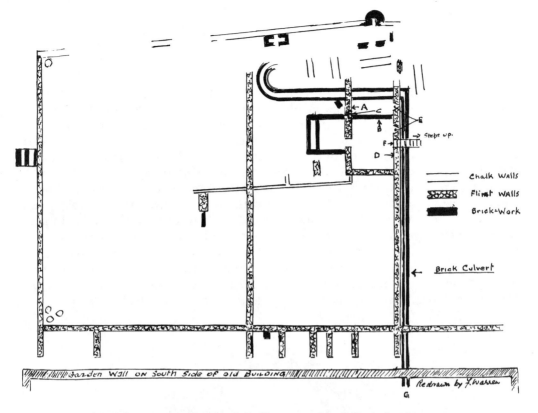

7. (*above*) Plan of the foundations (from an original drawn by the excavator, W.H. Mills, in 1912).
8. & 9. (*below*) Views of the uncovered walls (see text for explanation).

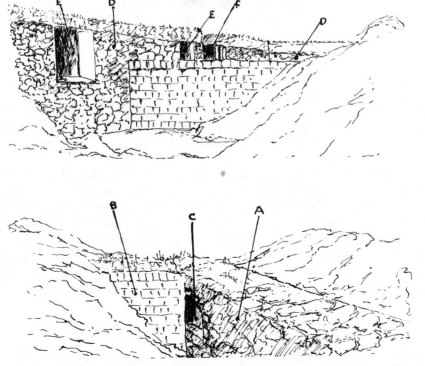

DRAWINGS RELATED TO ADDINGTON PLACE

manor-house, and during the development of the modern building site in Roxton Gardens, behind the church, an incident occurred which tended to confirm such a belief. It happened in 1963 when a subsidence revealed a pit or room in which was a large number of oyster or scallop shells. Legend has it that Henry VIII used the house as a hunting lodge in the first half of the 16th century, and if he did, then these shells could have been the debris of many a merry banquet, following upon the exertions and excitement of the chase. It has to be remembered, however, that the Leigh family held the manor during Henry's reign, and for a long time afterwards, and they, too, were likely to have entertained many notable guests, and to have fed them in right royal fashion. The shells were seen by Mr. and Mrs. Scott, who still live in the village road, and they reported that they were piled high, one on top of the other to form a kind of wall. This find was not allowed to be the subject of an archaeological examination, however, for the developers' plans for meeting completion dates had to be honoured.

10. A subterranean passage, discovered
by W. H. Mills in 1911

A third sketch from the pencil of Mr. Mills shows a section of an underground tunnel or passage found when he discovered the cellars in 1911. It was probably the southern end of the culvert shown against the eastern wall of the building on the plan made by him in 1912. Mills suggested that it was a drain for the disposal of waste from the manor-house. There is another such culvert—believed to have served a similar purpose—under the lawn at Addington Place—which runs under the golf course towards the church. It is possible that both channels were united at some point, perhaps above the circle of horse-chestnut trees in the recreation ground between Gravel Hill and the village of Addington. These trees were planted—so it has been said—to mask a cess-pit, perhaps the terminal point of the drainage system of the last two manor-houses of the ancient manor of Addington.

Dr. Herring, Archbishop of Canterbury from 1747 to 1757, was resident in the Old Palace at Croydon from time to time, and apparently visited Addington during his term as archbishop. He wrote a letter to Dr. Ducarel,[24] the one-time keeper of the library at Lambeth Palace, and although there is no record of when the letter was sent, it is known that Ducarel acknowledged its receipt on 16 January 1755. In the letter the archbishop informed Dr. Ducarel of '. . . an inscription over the door of Sir John Leigh's house at Addington'. The inscription was in the form of a verse, and has often been quoted in connection with the history of the manor. No apology is made for doing so again in these pages:

> In fourteen hundred and none
> Here was neither stick nor stone,
> In fourteen hundred and three
> The goodly building which you see.

It is surely inconceivable that the archbishop would have mentioned this piece of doggerel if he had not been certain that it was where he said it was. That must imply that he personally visited the house, although Sir John Leigh had died in 1737, some 17 years earlier. John Leigh's will was the subject of a long lawsuit after his death, and matters were not resolved until 1744, when the manor was awarded to two nieces of the deceased knight. Herring's use of the phrase—'the house of Sir John Leigh'—whether or not the visit was made before or after the knight's death, no doubt recognised the name by which the house was locally known. If the evidence presented by the archbishop is accepted, the house called Addington Place must have been built at the start of the 15th century, and must have been the Addington home of at least 10 of the local lords of the manor, from William Bardolph (1389-1424) to Sir John Leigh (1690-1737). Mr. Mills's statement that the walls were medieval would then seem to be correct. In an article on 'The Field Names of Addington' Mills wrote, 'The eastern side of Spout Hill, Addington, from a point opposite the "Lion Lodges" to the top of the Hill, has been known for many years as "Bardoll's or Bardolph's Bank".' Obviously it has been so called because of its association with the William Bardolph who is supposed to have built the house c. 1400-1403. Could the bank have been formed by the deposition of soil taken from inside the park when the old manor-house was being built? The Revd. Lysons in his *Environs of London,* and Edward Walford, compiler of *Greater London,* each describe the house as being built of flint and chalk, materials often seen in buildings erected in that period of England's history.

The histories written by Brayley, Lysons, Walford, and by the writers of the *Victoria County History of England,* have all recorded that a 'new house', replacing the legendary castle, was erected between 1400 and 1403. They also agree that the 'new house' was demolished in 1780. The only manor-house in Addington that was dealt with in that manner at that time was Addington Place, once the home of Sir John Leigh, but in 1780 vacated by a later holder of the property when the present Addington Palace was completed. The only reference to a specific house bearing the dates 1400–3 is that made by Archbishop Herring in 1754–55.

All the authorities mentioned—except Lysons—assert that the house was built on the same spot as the 'castle' it superseded. Walford quotes an article published in *The Gentleman's Magazine* in 1799[25] in which the church is mentioned as being one of the oldest in the county. The writer continued '. . . on an eminence adjoining, are the remains of a Monastery . . .'. Now, 'adjoining' means near, or next to: a definition surely applicable to the site behind the church. This extract from *The Gentleman's Magazine* was probably the source of the *Victoria County History's* reference to the 'remains of a medieval house' being seen in 1799. The statement that the remains were those of a monastery is probably incorrect, the similarity of the building materials used to those seen in the church, and to their evident medieval nature.

The *London Magazine* for 1782 had an article on Addington Place, described as the 'seat of James Trecothick'. That house was completed in 1780, and retained the old name until 1808, when it was bought for the Archbishops of Canterbury and given the title Addington Palace. The article went on to say that 'tradition puts the Castle near this spot'.

William Camden wrote in 1586,[26] 'Eastward of Croiden standeth Addington, habitation of Sir Olliff Leigh—whereby is to be seen the ruble of a Castle of Sir Robert Agyllon, and from him of the Lords Bardolph'. The association of the Aguillon and the Bardolph families with the Leighs has already been noted, and Olliff—or Olliphe-Leigh was the great-great-great-grandfather of the Sir John Leigh mentioned by Archbishop Herring in his letter to Dr. Ducarel, *c.* 1754–5. Olliphe-Leigh's house was, almost certainly, the mansion acquired by Barlow Trecothick in 1767 from the successors to Sir John Leigh. If Camden's 'whereby' can be equated with the words 'adjoining' and 'near' in the *London Magazine* and *The Gentleman's Magazine,* then the possibility that Aguillon's fortified mansion, the early 14th-century mansion-house of William Bardolph, and the house of Sir John Leigh, *c.* 1737, all stood on the same spot here behind the church cannot be ignored.

6. Kent Gate

There is one other site which must be considered. It is in the woodlands on the northern side of the village road, on the boundary between Kent and Surrey. Rocque shows the spot on his map of Surrey (*c.* 1760) where he indicates a building of some size and importance as standing here in the 18th century. Some historians have suggested that the structure might have been the Chapel of All Saints, said to have been included in the gift of Addington church to the church of St. Mary Overie at Southwark. Others have mentioned the legendary monastery and have associated the site with that supposed ecclesiastical edifice. There seems to be no documentary evidence which offers support to either theory. There is a chance that here, too, lie the remains of a manor-house, but in relation to the other sites mentioned earlier it seems to be rather unlikely. As has been said before, only an archaeological investigation can decide whether the spot holds any significant clues to the past history of Addington.

7. Addington Palace

11. Addington Palace, 1978. Formerly 'Addington Place', it became a 'Palace' in 1808. The upper storey was added after it became the home of the Archbishops of Canterbury

The last of the manor-houses to be the seat of manorial authority in the parish and village of Addington is the building we know as Addington Palace. The house is still standing, although its erstwhile importance as a manor-house was lost in the first decade of the present century. The house has since January 1954 been the home of the Royal School of Church Music, reminding us in some degree of the association of the building with the Archbishops of Canterbury, who were lords of the manor of Addington from 1808 to 1898. The mansion is, historically speaking, a modern structure, and as such, really outside the scope of this chapter. In the previous pages an effort has been made to identify all the likely sites on which the more ancient of Addington's important houses might have stood, and to correlate the statements of other writers on the subject. In addition to the above, notice has been taken of the work of Mr. W. H. Mills in locating the Birch Wood site, and of his collection of local historical information which is in the care of Croydon Reference Library. It is to be hoped that further archaeological explorations of the sites mentioned in the foregoing pages will be possible in the not too far distant future.

12. Another view of Addington Palace

Chapter Five

THE CHURCH OF ST MARY THE BLESSED VIRGIN

THE COMPILERS of the Domesday Book made no mention of a church in Addington, but that omission does not necessarily mean that such a building did not exist. They did not mention a house either, although the very presence of the manors to which they did refer implied that some such edifice must have stood in the 'demesne lands' mentioned in the Survey. However, it seems to have been accepted that the church was built, or at least its construction was begun, in A.D. 1080. The collection of material for inclusion in the Domesday Record was begun in that year, and it is possible that when King William's inquisitors arrived in Addington to begin their investigation the church was unfinished, and so was not recorded. The possibility that long before the Conqueror crossed the English Channel a Saxon church stood upon the site has been considered from time to time, but no evidence has so far been found to support the theory. Neither will modern visitors to St Mary's church in Addington observe much affinity with the architectural style of the 11th century. Extensive repairs and restorations, alterations and additions, have destroyed or hidden much of the original fabric, although some signs of its undoubted antiquity still exist.

It is probable that the chancel and the nave were erected at the same time, the dimensions of each being much the same as those of the present day. The material used was flint, which could be found in abundance in the fields south of the ancient track that was to become Addington Village Road. The structure was lit by small lancet windows. There were three in the chancel, one in the north wall now looking into the vestry, another opposite it in the south wall, and the third one was high up in the apex of the east wall. The glass now in these windows is of 19th-century workmanship, although that in the lancet in the north side may be older. Similar windows were probably set in the walls of the nave, but subsequent alterations and additions would have destroyed them. The trio of windows immediately behind the altar was inserted in 1140 and is of interest in that it is believed to be one of only two such groupings in the county of Surrey. The other is at Bletchingley. The first tower of Addington church was built in 1180, and was oblong rather than square, and not very high. Battlements were added at a later date.

The church was for many years in the Deanery of Ewell in Surrey, and Ewell was part of the Diocese of Winchester. The association of the local church with

13. The church of St Mary the Blessed Virgin, 1975

that particular see probably dates from its dedication in the 11th century. Certainly the transfer of the church to the Southwark church of St Mary Overie was influenced by Richard, Bishop of Winchester[1] in the late 12th century. It was at his petition that Bartholomew de Caisneto or de Chesnaye granted to the canons of St Mary, Southwark, the church of 'Edintona' (Addington) in 'Frank Almoign' (as a free gift to God or his people). The Charter was witnessed by Herbert, Archdeacon of Canterbury, Gilbert of Blanville, and others. The terms of the transfer gave to the London church the right to appoint their own nominees to Addington, and priests from Southwark continued to serve locally until the practice was ended by the dissolution of the monasteries by Henry VIII. One provision made in the terms under which the church was given to St Mary Overie was that a lamp was to be kept burning in the chancel of Addington church 'in perpetuity'. After the action taken by the king in the 16th century the custom was abandoned. The sanctuary lamp now hanging in the chancel was introduced in 1947, and is not connected in any way with the events of nearly 800 years ago. The long association of Addington with the Bishops of Winchester was ended when the parish was transferred to the Croydon Deanery and included in the see of Canterbury in 1837.

The first major works of repair and reconstruction were carried out in 1210 after the roof of the chancel had fallen in, and the east wall was found to be in danger of collapse. The wall was repaired and a new roof was fitted, and during these operations the lancet windows in the east and south walls were filled in. A new larger window was inserted in the south wall, and another lancet was placed towards the western end of the wall. The narrow south aisle was added to the nave, and this involved the erection of the four pillars—two octagonal and two cylindrical—which support three plain, pointed arches. It will be noticed that the bases of these ancient pillars are not visible above floor level, and this fact has occasioned speculation as to whether the church has 'sunk very low' as John Aubrey suggested in his *Perambulation of the County of Surrey* (published 1719), or whether the floor has been considerably raised since the aisle was built. The last seems to be the more likely explanation. The increase in the overall width of the church as a result of the construction of the aisle caused an alteration in the external appearance of the building. The existing slope of the roof of the nave was maintained over the new aisle, the roof—again quoting Aubrey— 'descending very low'.

The 'low side window' was introduced into the chancel in 1350, set below the 13th-century lancet to which reference has already been made. Outwardly the two are separate features, but internally the window casings are merged, although they are marginally out of centre with one another. Only the inner half of the pointed trefoil opening can be called ancient, the outer portion having been restored with Bath stone.[2] The iron bars on the inside—or at least the round ones —are old, possibly coeval with the window itself. The sill is wide, and set about 18 ins. from the floor, ideal for use as a seat upon which a priest might sit when hearing confessions. The window case was originally grooved, suggesting that a shutter was once present. This could be closed to preserve the anonymity of penitents, or opened to allow the elements of the sacraments to be passed to those suffering from the dreaded disease of leprosy.

In 1773 a programme of restoration was initiated and financed by the then lord of the manor, Barlow Trecothick. Repairs were made to the tower and to the main walls, some of the original flint being replaced with brick. The raising of the walls of the south aisle, the provision of a new roof, and the insertion of the large window to the right of the porch and the lancets at each end of the aisle were almost certainly part of the work done at the time. When all was finished the outside of the building was stuccoed. A sketch showing the south aisle with the walls at their present height is to be seen in the *Victoria County History of England (Surrey)*, Vol. 4, p. 166, and another drawing, giving much

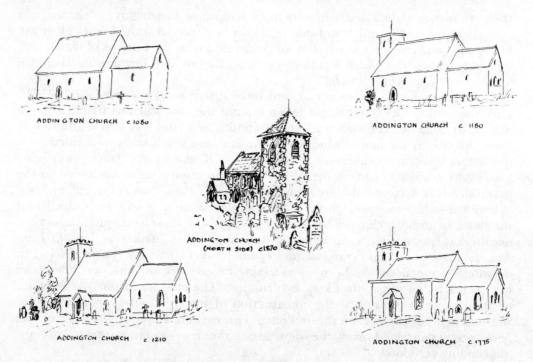

ADDINGTON CHURCH c 1080

ADDINGTON CHURCH c 1180

ADDINGTON CHURCH
(NORTH SIDE) c1870

ADDINGTON CHURCH c 1210

ADDINGTON CHURCH c 1775

14. The development of the church building over the centuries

the same view of the church, was published in a work called *100 Views of Surrey Churches* in 1827. Included in the last-mentioned sketch are two cottages to the east of the church, standing on land which now forms the eastern extension of the churchyard.

Dr. Charles Manners-Sutton came to Addington after the manor and mansion had been bought for the Archbishops of Canterbury in 1808. He was the first prelate to live in the place, and the first to be buried in Addington church. Before his death he had obtained permission for the construction of a vault under the floor of the small vestry that had been built against the original north wall of the church. He died in July 1828 and was buried in the place which he himself had prepared as a last resting place. His son, also named Charles, was Speaker of the House of Commons from 1817, and he lies in the same vault. The position of the burial place in relation to present conditions in the church is a spot some three to four feet from the vestry door, and between six and seven feet south of the organ enclosure.

Application was made in 1817 for a faculty permitting the erection of a gallery across the full width of the nave at its western end. From 1837 it was used by the organist and the choir. Access to the gallery was by a door under the structure which led into the tower, and from there a flight of steps led up into the gallery.

The 'Kynnersley Stone' on the floor of the nave (partially covered by pews and a radiator), would have been across the gallery doorway.

The second of the archbishops to reside in the building we know as Addington Place was William Howley. During his term as archbishop he provided the church with a new porch which is still in use. A new font was also installed, and the old seats were replaced with new 'backed' pews, which enabled the seating capacity to be increased to two hundred and sixty. The interior walls were cleaned and whitewashed and the outer walls were repaired and then refaced with flint, so restoring in some measure at least the ancient appearance of the church. A monument to Archbishop Howley is in an alcove in the north wall of the chancel at its eastern end. A recumbent figure originally represented the deceased prelate, but this was removed to Canterbury and the present cross placed on the tomb instead. A tablet set high up on the chancel arch and facing east records that the remains of Archbishop Howley, with those of his wife, two of his sons and an infant grandson are 'deposited in the vaults beneath'. A brass plate set in the floor of the nave at the centre of the crossing also commemorates William Howley and his wife, Mary Frances.

The largest and most impressive of the monuments to be seen in the chancel is that to members of the Leigh family, lords of the manor of Addington for about 300 years. It was erected by Sir Francis Leigh of Addington, c. 1613/4 in accordance with the wishes of his father, Sir Olliphe Leigh, who died in 1612. Above a recumbent figure of Sir Olliphe are two alcoves, the one on the left holding representations of his parents, the right-hand recess having similar kneeling figures to commemorate his grandparents. The recumbent figure of a lady was added later. The carving represents Lady Jane Leigh, wife of Sir Olliphe, and mother of Sir Francis Leigh, who died in 1631. Originally there was a cornice bearing angels blowing trumpets, and pieces of armour (funerary ornaments) were hung on brackets on the wall above. Angels, trumpets, even the cornice itself, had all vanished when John Aubrey visited Addington at the end of the 17th century. The armour, plus some shields bearing the arms of the Leigh family were removed by persons unknown within the last 70 or 80 years.

On the floor below the Leigh monument is a brass to the memory of John Leigh, great-grandfather of Sir Olliphe Leigh. The inscription in the border gives the date of John Leigh's death wrongly as 1509. He actually died in 1503, as we know from his will and records of a post-mortem enquiry registered at Canterbury.[3] This brass was once part of a tomb which stood where the Howley monument now is, and it was placed in the present position to allow the archbishop's memorial to be installed. John Leigh's widow remarried more than once, but outlived all her husbands. She asked that her body should lie with that of her first husband and she was buried with him in the family vault below the chancel. Another brass is on the south side of the chancel and is to the memory of Thomas Hatteclyff, a Master of the Household of Henry VIII.

15. The Leigh family memorial in the church

A monument commemorating Alderman Barlow Trecothick of London stands
against the south wall above the Hatteclyff brass. When it was first set up in the
chancel it was placed behind the altar, obscuring the light from the centre
window. After over 60 years in that position it was moved to its present site.

The marble reredos was built at the end of the 19th century as a memorial
to Archbishop Benson (1881–1896). The alabaster figures represent four archbishops: Cranmer, Theodore, Benson, and Laud.[4] The chancel was decorated in

further recognition of the esteem in which Archbishop Benson was held. On the south wall are the coats of arms of the prelates buried at Addington, that of Benson being seen in the centre of the east wall. Another shield bearing the Benson arms can be seen above the Leigh monument. Other shields, representing Mary, the mother of Jesus, on the left of the east wall, and St Catherine of Alexandria on the extreme right, are part of the decoration. So, too, are two painted panels depicting—on the north wall—St Damian, and opposite—on the south wall—St Cosmas.

The display of the heraldic emblems of the archbishops is explained by their close assocation with Addington between 1808 and 1898. The reasons for the inclusion of the other symbols, and for the representations of Theodore, Cranmer, and Laud are less obvious. Theodore was archbishop in the 7th century when the decentralisation of ecclesiastical administration is thought to have begun. From that act of devolution the establishment of parochial units became commonplace. The parish of Addington no doubt stemmed from the work begun by Theodore, although his name does not appear in the annals of local history. Laud is mentioned once, when he wrote a letter to Sir Francis Leigh charging him to redress a wrong done to the then vicar, one James Lesley. Cranmer, like Theodore, seems to have had no direct connection with the church of Addington. The church is dedicated to Mary, the Blessed Virgin, and that might be thought to be reason enough to include the symbol of the 'pierced heart' in the upper left-hand corner of the east wall and perhaps, the mother and child seen in a shield above the Leigh memorial. St Catherine was martyred in Alexandria in the 4th century, and Damian and Cosmas were physicians of the same period. Since the formation of parishes did not begin until A.D. 668 the presence of panels containing representations of them is indeed surprising. However, Canon Benham (vicar 1867-1873) writing in 1877,[5] mentioned the will of a member of the Leigh family dated 1511. In this document bequests were made to 'the High Altar of Addington Church, 12 pence for forgotten tithes; to our ladye Altar, 6 pence; to Saint Kateryn auter 6 pence; and to the auter of Cosmo and Damiane 6 pence'.[6] Benham said that small altars were often to be found in churches similar to St Mary's, Addington. Perhaps the designers of the mural decorations in the chancel had access to Canon Benham's writings and so incorporated these apparently irrelevant symbols in the memorial to Archbishop Benson.

There are many other memorials in the church, too many to be described individually in these pages, but all are interesting. The windows at the western end of the building are in memory of Archbishop Tait and his son, Crauford Tait. A stained glass window in the south aisle is to the memory of Sir George Johnson, Physician Extraordinary to Queen Victoria, and is 'signed' with the golden 'garb' (wheatsheaf) of Charles Kemp, a noted specialist designer and craftsman in stained glass windows.

The present tower, the north aisle, the organ chamber,[7] and the vestry were added to the building in the years 1875/6, the architect being Mr. Piers

St Aubyns. The tower now holds six bells, two being added in 1957. Of the other four, two are unmarked, one has the date 1655 upon it, and one is inscribed: 'Christopher Hodson made me 1683'. An inventory of church goods, dated 1546,[8] includes an item recording that there were 'iij bells in the steepul', so it is certain that the sound of the bells of St Mary's have echoed across the woods and fields of this ancient parish for over 430 years.

Prior to the extensions to the church in the last quarter of the 19th century the appearance of the building, both inside and out, was very different from that seen today. To begin with, there was no north aisle, and only a small vestry on the north side of the church. The pulpit was against the north-west corner of the chancel, and a reading desk with a 'seat for the Clerk' stood against the old north wall. There was a door near the centre of the wall which led into the churchyard. The organ and the choir were accommodated in the gallery to which reference has already been made. That feature was removed in the general alterations made in the 1870s. The font installed by Archbishop Howley had replaced one which had stood at the western end of the nave near the pillars of the south aisle. John Aubrey saw that font in 1672 or thereabouts and described it as '. . . rather a pedestal to place a basin on—its cavity is so small it seems by accident rather than choice'.[9] An earlier font stood by the church door. The present font and baptistry were presented to the parish in 1913 by the then vicar, the Revd. Arthur Carr.

A sketch by Mr. W. H. Mills, made in 1872,[10] shows the old tower and the north wall with the vestry provided by Archbishop Manners-Sutton. The door mentioned above is shown and three windows appear in the upper half of the wall. The one in the centre may have been in the original 11th-century building, lighting the nave as the other lancets lit the chancel.

There have been 57 known incumbents of the parish of Addington, and a list of their names is hanging in the church. Unfortunately the records for various periods between 1080 and 1664 have been lost, and the figure of 57 given above probably represents about a half of the total number of priests who have officiated here. The parish registers, started in 1559, bear witness to the services rendered by many ministers to the people of Addington over more than four centuries. A few of them are worthy of recall: for instance, Thomas Berington. He was appointed to the living by no less a person than King Henry VIII, but by the time Edward VI was on the throne Berington was in arrears with the payment of tithes due to the king. When reminded of his obligation he refused to pay, and Edward VI deprived him of his benefice. Later it was revealed by the church-wardens that 'in the fyrst yere of the reyne of our Lord the King that now is . . . these parcelles folowing were imbesyled, sold and taken away out of the said Churche by one Sir Tomas Berington late Vicar of the Parish who is now ded and nothing worth at his death. Item: A vestment of dornixe with garters; ij [2] Alter Clothes; iiij [4] candilsticks of laten; a branche of laten for v [5] candiles; ij [2] candelsticks of laten y^t were before ye Trinitye; a lampe of laten;

THE CHURCH OF THE BLESSED VIRGIN MARY

a holy water stoke; a canopy with iij hops [? hoops] of laten; and a rude clothe with xij [12] apostelles paynted'.[11]

James Lesley, vicar from 1628 to 1652 was also concerned with the payment of tithes, not due from him to the king, but owed to the vicar by the lord of the manor, Sir Francis Leigh. Lesley also claimed that Leigh had illegally enclosed church lands and diminished the value of the living by so doing. James Lesley had the support of Archbishop Laud, but lost his claims after Leigh had appealed to the king. This vicar is also remembered for his eccentricity over the site of his wife's grave. He had buried her body in the south aisle of the church, placing a ledger stone across the entrance to the building. He is said to have taken special care to avoid stepping on the stone whenever he entered or left the church. The stone was removed from the aisle during one of the periods in which repairs were made to the building, and was lost for some years. It was 'rescued—from the stokehold',[12] by Mr. Mylne, vicar from 1884 to 1895, who had it set in its present position in the porch, to the right of the door.

The parishes of Addington and Shirley were united under one vicar between 1843 and 1867. He was Matthew Thomas Farrer who took a great interest in the education of the children of both districts. The successor to Matthew Farrer was Canon William Benham, of whose interest in matters relating to the history of Addington has already been mentioned. He wrote on one occasion of the crypt under the chancel, describing it as 'one huge arched vault'. He saw the wall erected by Barlow Trecothick to confine the remains of the Leigh family to the south side, and had part of the upper courses of brick removed in order that he might see what lay behind it. His own words best describe what was revealed: 'there was a confused heap, almost reaching to the roof of the vault, of bones and broken coffins'.

Electricity replaced candles as the source of illumination in the church at the end of the 1920s. It was installed through the generosity of Mr. and Mrs. William Cash. Mr. Cash held a prominent post in the management of the old Croydon Gas Company.

The Vestry

The present vestry contains some interesting portraits of the archbishops who lived in Addington during the 19th century. There are also portraits of the vicars of the parish from Matthew Farrer (1843-1867) to Arthur Carr (1895-1915). Parish clerks are not often mentioned. The earliest name is that of 'Walter' and the date given for him is 1314. Henry Lomas or Lamas was 'Clarke' in 1612, a William Howard held the post in the first decade of the 18th century, and the last person to act in that capacity was Stephen Pallmarine, who buried four Archbishops of Canterbury and died in 1895, aged 83 years.

The Churchyard

The yew tree to the west of the entrance to Addington churchyard was mentioned in a book called *Yew Trees of Great Britain and Ireland,* a work published in 1897. There is no doubt that the Addington yew is very old, although estimates of its age have varied considerably. The idea that it might date from the time of Edward the Confessor is perhaps a little unlikely, but it is known that the yew is a native of these islands, and that the species was present in some profusion in the Middle Ages. According to a modern expert on the subject the date of the planting of the tree is 'certainly not later than 1520', and probably 'around' 1450. That assessment places the age of the Addington yew at about 520 years. There is another yew tree in the churchyard, a few yards east of the gateway, and this is a younger tree, probably by as much as 200 years.

The most prominent memorial to be seen is the 20ft.-high cross presented and dedicated by Archbishop Randall Davidson in 1911. It was erected in memory of the five Archbishops of Canterbury who were buried in Addington. Two of them, as has been noted in previous pages, were buried in the vaults of the church. The other three lie in the churchyard. The site of John Bird Sumner's grave is against the north-eastern wall, surrounded by a low iron railing. Archbishop Tait is buried almost directly westward of the tower, and Charles Thomas Longley's grave is almost on the edge of the churchyard near the parish hall. When the foundations for this cross were being prepared, the remains of an old wall were found. It appeared that the wall ran north-westerly across the churchyard, and this would seem to indicate that the burial ground was once considerably smaller than it is at present. A tablet in the vestry which records a gift of 'glebe' land for the extension of the churchyard tells us that the donor was the Revd. M. T. Farrer, and that he made the gift in 1849. The Addington tithe map, *c.* 1842, shows a building, probably a barn, which could have stood near the wall which might have been seen before the churchyard was enlarged, and long before the erection of the memorial to the archbishops.

The wall on the eastern side of the churchyard, against which lie the graves of members of Archbishop Sumner's family, once continued southwards to the village road. Part of the wall was removed to enable the churchyard to be extended to make room for more burials. The ground gained by that operation had, for the greater part of the 19th century and for the early years of the 20th, a pair of cottages standing upon it. A further extension of the burial ground was made after the Second World War, using ground that had once been part of the Home Farm attached to the ancient manor house of the Leigh family.

From an inventory of graves compiled by the late W. H. Mills, and dated 1908, it is possible to select a few wherein lie the remains of some of the better-known families who have worked and worshipped in Addington.

To the right of the porch and near the south aisle are several graves bearing the names of Howard, Joyner, Bullock, and Ovenden. These families have between them provided many hosts of the village inn, and from the menfolk especially, many members of Addington's cricket club, which has a history going back for more than two centuries. Also near the porch are stones marking the graves of the Covell family. The name is also to be seen in the earliest register of the parish of Addington in 1559!

Close by, but nearer to the roadway, is the grave of Thomas Meager, bearing the date 1699. The Meagers were a very old family in this part of Surrey. They farmed land on the north side of Oaks Road, Shirley, and also had land in Coombe and Croydon. Although the Meager stone bears the earliest date still to be seen in the churchyard today, the oldest grave is thought to be under the old yew tree. It is marked by an old, half-buried stone, black with age, its inscription eroded by long exposure to the elements. The earliest date suggested for this grave is 1593. Another estimate suggested 1630 as the probable date. Whether it is really the oldest grave in this ancient graveyard will probably never be known for certain, but its weather-worn sunken surface encourages the belief that it might well be deserving of that title.

The name of Coppin has already been mentioned in this history, and it can be traced in the records of the births, marriages and deaths of the family written in the pages of the parish registers from the time of King Charles I to the present century. Among the farmers who have tilled the lands of Addington and now lie in the quiet of the churchyard many well-known families are represented. The names of White and Walker, Fuller and Field, Cooper and Brabiner and Still appear frequently on the gravestones. Other names, of shepherds, stockmen, and farm hands of every kind, of tradesmen, craftsmen, and gamekeepers are here beside the others, names like Alexander, Blundell, Chapell, Drewett, Dubery, Dedman, Knowlson and Scott. It is, of course, impossible to mention every grave and every personality lying in this churchyard, and there are many which have been omitted. Such omissions carry no condemnation of any names unmentioned, all of whom by their very presence in the community contributed greatly to the continuing history of Addington.

Chapter Six

ADDINGTON VILLAGE

ALTHOUGH THE CHURCH does not look particularly ancient there is no doubt that it is the oldest building in the village. Second place in any table of antiquity may belong to Addington House, Spout Hill. This building has some 15th-century work in it, added to in the 17th and 18th centuries. It can best be seen from The Wicket, a modern road on the western edge of the Cricket Green, off the Village Road.

The smithy, thought to have its historical roots in the 16th century, may be older, although whether it can actually claim seniority over Addington House is somewhat doubtful. The old forge has been used by the blacksmiths of Addington for more than 350 years, and perhaps the best-known name among those connected with that ancient craft is that of the Coppin family. They came with the Huguenots from France and settled in the south-eastern part of England. The name was then spelt 'Cophin' which gradually became changed into Coppin. Members of the original immigrant families who lived in West Wickham acquired a 'g', being called Copping. In Croydon the name became Coppin. The Addington family of Coppin not only established themselves as blacksmiths; they were also numbered among the parish clerks, and held positions as churchwardens for many years.

One of them was the last parish constable to be appointed by the parish council before that authority was taken away from them. His name was William, and he held office c. 1830–40. He had been born lame and had to wear a special boot. This caused him to make a noise when he walked and earned him the nickname of 'Bonker' Coppin. In later life when he had become the local policeman, he was often seen walking on Castle Hill, both on and off duty. The hill became known as 'Bonker's Knob' because of his obvious liking for the spot. The euphemism is currently seen in the name given to a public house in the Fieldway district of New Addington, but the name is mis-spelt *Bunker's Knob*.

The last member of the family to follow his ancestors as a blacksmith was Leslie Coppin, in the early years of the present century. He was not only skilled in the working of iron and the shoeing of horses, but was an inventor as well. Among his ideas for improving the tools of the agricultural workers was a design for a long tree-pruner which had apparently not been thought of before. He invented detachable points for harrows, enabling them to be taken off for

16. The village smithy, over 300 years old

sharpening without dismantling the whole harrow. A 'pneumatic pad' for horses' hooves was another of his ideas. He had the reputation of being too generous where his patents were concerned, either giving them away or selling them for next to nothing. Many were allowed to lapse. One of his patents was sold for five shillings! It was for a bicycle with wheels of equal size, an idea which has been credited to Lord Nuffield, who turned a bicycle business into the Morris Motor Company.

The *Cricketers Inn* as it stands today is the result of alterations and additions made in the last two decades, i.e., since 1950. The building was erected in 1844, replacing a much more ancient inn which had stood behind the present house for over 250 years. The name 'Cricketers' probably dates from the formation of the first Addington cricket club in 1743. On 5 July in that year an eleven from Addington played the London cricket club on the Artillery ground (Hon. Artillery Company) at Finsbury, and won by an innings and four runs. Two years later the two teams met again on Addington Hills when the local team was again victorious. The game has continued to flourish in Addington until the present day, but the present Cricket Meadow has only been used for the last 100 years or so.

17. The *Cricketers Inn*, *c.*1914.

A bat said to have been used by a former landlord of the inn towards the end of the 18th century still hangs in the *Cricketers Inn*. Before the coming of England's favourite summer game, the earlier inn mentioned above had been called *The Three Lions,* the name having reference to the arms borne by the Leigh family, the last of the truly hereditary lords of the manor of Addington.

The Still family were well known and respected for many years in the local community. In 1867 Henry Still left his father's farm in Chelsham to take over two farms centred on the village of Addington. These had been cultivated as one unit from the year 1817, when William and Edmund White had held them from Archbishop Manners-Sutton, first of the archbishops to hold the ancient manor of the Leighs. One of the farms was known as Lower House Farm, its farmhouse, farmyard and ancillary buildings occupying ground between Lodge Lane, the old Addington Village Road, and the modern Kent Gate Way. The other farm had Addington House as its administrative centre, and its farmyard, cowsheds, stables and barns on the Village Road between Spout Hill and the Cricket Meadow. The combined areas covered the ground of Addington from the border with Kent to the Addington–Selsdon boundary. The land included fields on either side of the Village Road, and on both sides of Featherbed Lane and Selsdon Park Road. The houses of the Forestdale housing development now cover the last-mentioned site. For many years sheep were predominant on the farms of Addington, but in later years they were superseded by pedigree herds of Friesian cattle and a greater acreage was put under cereals and other crops.

The present Castle Hill Avenue at New Addington marks the southern boundary of another of Addington's ancient farms. The farmhouse was demolished when the land was developed in the years after the 1939–45 War. It stood in Lodge

Lane, just north of the entrance to Headley Drive. The farm took its name from
the hillside on which it stood, and Castle Hill itself is traditionally linked with the
legendary castle of Baron Robert Aguillon who lived in Addington in 1270-1.
Opposite the site of the farmhouse is a field known for very many years as Mill
Field. The existence of a mill in Addington in the early part of the 14th century
was mentioned in an inventory made in relation to the estates of Hugh Bardolph,
son-in-law of and successor to Robert Aguillon. It could well have been erected
in the field just described. Whether or not Castle Hill Farm ever had any direct
connection with Aguillon's castle or with Bardolph's mill has never been
positively established. In the 1890s the farm was taken over by Henry Still from
the then owners, the Lennard family of Wickham Court in Kent. He added it
to his other farmlands, his son, W. H. Still, living in the newly-acquired farmhouse.

Churchgoers and cricketers alike have cause to remember the names of Henry,
W. H., and Brian Still. Farmers of many acres for more than 100 years, they also
served the church. Henry was churchwarden for many years; his son—William
Henry Still— was church organist for more than 60 years, and his son, Brian W. N.
Still, J.P., was deputy to his father and also a chorister for most of his life. It is
to the elder of the three that our thanks are due for the Cricket Meadow. It is
not known if he played for the local team, but his son, W. H. Still, certainly did.
He was captain of the side for over 50 years. Brian Still was also captain of the
cricket club, and a valued member of the team.

Beyond the southern edge of Castle Hill Farm and extending over the rest of
New Addington were the fields of Addington Lodge Farm. The administrative
centre of this agricultural area was a farmhouse situated on the western side of
the farm, behind a road now called Northdown Crescent. The highways department of the London Borough of Croydon now use the house as a depot. In
1317 the farm was apparently in the hands of Sir Walter de Huntingfield of
Wickham, who was licensed to 'impark' certain areas of woodland.[1] A John de
Bures is known to have held the Addington Lodge area in 1353 when he sold
his manor to a Mr. Winkeworth.[2] Sir Olliphe Leigh held the territory in 1612,[3]
although the farming rights were held by a tenant farmer, Thomas Wood, a
native of Coulsdon. In 1753 the farmer was Thomas Brazier, who was waylaid
and robbed while on his way home from Croydon market. A more modern
reference to the manorial status of the area is seen in a Bill presented to
parliament in 1797 allowing the 'inclosure' of certain lands in the parish of
Croydon. James Trecothick of Addington Place claimed relief from the
provisions of the Bill as 'owner of the Manors of Addington Temple, Bardolph,
and Bures'. It has already been suggested in an earlier chapter of this work that
this southern part of the parish of Addington might have been part of the
Domesday manor of Albert the Clerk. If that be the case, the manor-house of
John de Bures might have stood where the highways depot stands today. Only
an archaeological investigation will establish the facts, and perhaps such an
examination will be possible in the years to come.

Returning to the village and the *Cricketers Inn,* there is on the opposite side of the road the remains of an avenue. In the 18th and 19th centuries it linked the Village Road with the main carriage drive from the Lion Lodges in Spout Hill to either Addington Place or Addington Palace. The former stood behind the church; the latter is still standing, on the other side of the park grounds. The drive was flanked by a double row of elm trees on either side, and the remnants of that once splendid avenue can still be seen from the greens of the Addington Palace golf course. The house opposite the inn on the Village Road was part of a complex of farm buildings belonging to the Home Farm which served the domestic needs of the palace and of the old manor-house which was demolished *c.* 1780.

The barn by the recreation ground has recently been repaired and re-roofed, and is now used by the staff of the golf club. It is probably 18th century, but it could be older. A 'terrific' storm broke over Addington on 2 May 1815. During a two-hour ordeal of torrential rain much damage was done to livestock on the Home Farm, some pigs being swept away and drowned. A barn on the site of the present church hall was totally destroyed and the walls of the churchyard were broken down. Gravestones were washed from their places and coffins exposed. The *Cricketers'* cellars were flooded, casks and barrels of liquor were lifted up against the floor above and bursting through it, floated off along the Village Road. The landlord's small daughter was saved by her nurse, who climbed with the child on to the top of a farm wagon. Horses were immersed in water up to their necks, but, fortunately, no human lives were lost.[4]

Addington's first and only village store was built on the corner of the Village Road and Lodge Lane in 1881. It was a co-operative enterprise, with shares at five shillings each held by the 'founding members', among whom could be numbered the more prominent residents of Addington. The total number of shares was 400, of which 250 were offered at the price mentioned above, the remainder being available to the villagers at two shillings and sixpence a time.[5]

The premises were opened in October 1881, under the management of Mr. Inkpen. It was estimated that the weekly takings would be about £10, and by February 1882 the receipts had reached £16 a week. A bonus of ninepence in the pound was paid to members, calculated on the value of the purchases made. 'Hosiery and Drapery' goods were added to the articles on sale in 1884. In September of that year the letter-box that had been in the churchyard wall was removed and a new pillar-box provided outside the store. Mr. Adams, the manager, was appointed postmaster, and Addington had its own post office.

When the building was erected the western half was set aside for the trading activities, and the eastern half contained living quarters for a curate. He combined his duties as assistant to the vicar with the responsibilities of a 'Youth Leader', a room for recreation being provided on the ground floor of that part of the building. The co-operative nature of the business ended between the two World Wars, and the store came under private enterprise. All the post office facilities

18. The village store, built in 1881

were transferred to other premises in Selsdon Park Road in the 1960s, and when the new roundabout in Lodge Lane was under construction the shop closed its doors for the last time. The 90-year-old building is now a private residence.

The farms in and to the south of the village have now been dealt with, but there were other farms in other parts of the ancient parish of Addington. Immediately to the north of the old manorial park, across the present Shirley Church Road, is an area once known as Spring Park Farm. The territory is bounded on the north by the road to Wickham, and was originally part of a large area of common land which included Addington and Shirley commons, which were themselves an extension of Addington Hills. The farmhouse from which this farm was administered was built in the early years of the reign of Queen Anne. The site of the building was at the end of Farm Drive, a short road leading from Bridle Road, Shirley. Beyond the end of Farm Drive, the old farm road still remains as a path running between and parallel to Bennetts Way and Devonshire Way, Shirley.

In 1812 the farm was run by a Colonel John Maberley, of Shirley House, demolished to enable the Trinity School of John Whitgift to be built. Attached to the home of John Maberley was Shirley Park Farm, sometimes called Oaks Farm, and this was managed in conjunction with Spring Park Farm. The colonel was very interested in hunting and maintained kennels belonging to the Old Surrey Foxhounds at his own expense. The Addington tithe map of 1842 shows a field adjacent to Shirley Church Road marked 'Kennel Piece', and it is not unlikely that this was where the hounds were kept. The colonel was adjudged bankrupt in 1834. His successor was John Temple Leader, who let the land to

Mr. Hewitt Davies. Davies was not afraid to experiment with new crops, and is said to have been the first farmer to introduce 'white wheat' into England. Between 1923 and 1939 an extensive housing programme was started, and by the start of the Second World War the fields of Spring Park Farm were covered with houses.

Beyond Wickham Road to the north there is an area of land known as Monks Orchard. Legend tells of Plantagenet kings hunting in the woods that covered the territory in the Middle Ages. It has been noted by some historians that the armorial crest of King Richard II was a white hart, and that there is at the south-eastern corner of Monks Orchard a public house bearing the same name. From that coincidence, it is inferred that Richard was one of the kings mentioned above, perhaps pausing to drink in some contemporary hostelry on the same site!

The name 'Monk' in connection with this northernmost part of the parish of Addington is thought to be a modern version of the name mentioned in the 16th century. In a 'declaration of ye utter bownds of the Manor of Croydon' ordered by Archbishop Cranmer in 1552, part of the boundary between Upper Elmers End and Wickham Road is described as 'boundinge uppon Munkes Mead' and it would seem that the change from 'Munkes' to Monks is due to a natural corruption of the original spelling over the years.

Monks Orchard Farm (alias Monks Farm, West Shirley Farm, or Park Farm) was owned in the early years of the 19th century by Paul James le Cointe who died in 1825 and is buried in Addington church. He was followed by Samuel Jones Loyd who later became Lord Overstone. The old house was pulled down by his nephew, Lewis Loyd, and a new one built. This, too, was removed in 1928, and the Queen Mary's Homes were erected on the site. These are now incorporated with the Bethlem Royal Hospital which now occupies the old estate of Monks Orchard.

The boundary between the Addington and Croydon Manors mentioned above goes on from the Wickham Road via Spring Park Road to Shirley Church Road, then by a pathway to Sandpits Road and on behind the *Sandrock Hotel* at Shirley; then through the woods on the south side of Oaks Road to Coombe Lane. This road comes from Croydon and continues up the hill between Addington Hills on the left, and the Ballards Plantation on the right. Cranmer's records of Croydon's boundaries calls the last-mentioned area 'Priors Ballards', and this has led to the assumption that the land was once held by the London church of St Mary Overie, for that church sent many of its priests to serve in parishes in this part of Surrey. The upper parts of the estate were, like the top of Addington Hills, areas covered with heather, and it has been said that the name 'Ballards' came from the 'baldness' of the terrain. There is, however, an alternative suggestion as to the origin of this name. In the early 17th century Sir Olliphe Leigh of Addington manor also held the manor of Croham, with Croham Farm. This was a long way from Addington and was managed by a bailiff. Servants of Sir Olliphe sent to Croham would have passed through the

Ballards Estate as they went 'towards the Bailiff', or as Addington villagers would say, 'Baileywards', which became 'Ballards' by repeated utterance of the phrase. The association of the Croham property with Sir Olliphe Leigh lasted only a few years and the last-mentioned theory as to the origins of the name 'Ballards' is hardly likely to be correct.

Before 1813 the property was in the hands of Robert Wylie, and in 1817 William Coles of Heathfield held it. About 1822 Charles Piescal Hoffman was the owner, with Augustus Hoffman, his uncle, as guardian. That family continued in residence until 1870. The estate was bought c. 1872-3 by Charles H. Goschen, who built a new mansion at the top of the hill. He called his new house St Andrews. The family remained in possession until 1919, and in the following year the estate was bought by a well-known Croydon figure, Howard Houlder. The appellation 'Ballards Plantation' dates from the end of the 19th century when the erstwhile 'bare' heights were planted with trees.

There was a farm on the southern side of the property, called 'Ballard's Farm'. It maintained a large dairy herd and ran its own milk delivery service. It was flourishing during the 18th and 19th centuries and lasted until the 1950s. Part of the land is covered with houses, and the rest is incorporated in the main estate, which is now the site of a large educational establishment.

Heathfield Farm lies between Ballards Way and Selsdon Park Road, and stretches from Gravel Hill to Foxearth Wood in Selsdon. On 6 November 1629, close to midnight, two men set out to cross the area known today as Monks Hill, then part of the Heathfield estate. The night was dark and a gale force wind was blowing heavy rain across the ground. The story goes that when the morning came, one of them lay dead upon the ground; he was a priest who had been murdered by a 'foreigner' from Croydon. That, so it is said, is how Monks Hill got its name. Parish records, however, show that it was the priest who did the killing. It is very unlikely that the incident led to the naming of the hill. The name 'Monk' is seen many times in the church registers, and it is probable that Monks Hill was owned at one time by a person named Monk. It is also unlikely that such a person was connected in any way with the 'Munke' mentioned in reference to Monks Orchard.

The farm, of which the hill was but a part, was known in the 18th century as 'Stones Farm', probably because of the stony nature of the soil. Heathfield, like Ballards, is part of the Addington Hills formation, and was likely to have exhibited some similarity of soil conditions. The name was changed to the present title in 1823 when the territory was held by a Mr. William Coles, under lease from the archbishops. Later, the property was controlled by Henry Goschen, Esq., who was very interested in the affairs of Addington. He was a churchwarden, a lay preacher, and for over 40 years a chorister at the parish church. He died in 1922 and was buried at Addington. The house and gardens, together with the farm were then bought by R. E. A. Riesco, Esq. After he died the house was bought by Croydon Council, and it is now used by the Education Department as a Science and Geography Resources Area. The grounds are now open to the public.

The hamlet of Addington Hills consisted of about twenty cottages which stood on either side of Shirley Hills Road between the *Sandrock Hotel* and the top of the hill. Most of them were of flint and were still standing in the 1890s. A mission chapel was provided in November 1873, the foundation stone having been laid in the previous August by Archbishop Tait. An infants' school in the same building was opened on 13 April 1874. There were a few more cottages in Oaks Road which were part of the hamlet of Addington Hills. They were known as the 'Alwen' cottages and belonged to the Alwen family, who operated the windmill that can still be seen in the grounds of John Ruskin School, Shirley. Its sails have not turned since the end of the last century. The cottage nearest to the entrance to Badger's Hole was noted for the example of topiary to be found in its carefully tended garden. All the cottages were standing until 1935 or 1936. Although the Alwens were 'Shirley' folk, several members of the family lie in Addington churchyard, in graves near the church tower.

Badger's Hole almost certainly got its name from the fact that it was the home of large numbers of badgers. The sandy nature of the soil and the furze and coarse grass that grew there made the place eminently suitable for this particular animal. During the 18th and 19th centuries many Londoners came here to indulge in the sport of badger baiting, and also to set up arenas wherein their fighting cocks could do battle, while wagers were laid on the results.

There was once an inn or ale-house in Badger's Hole. It was, not surprisingly, called *The Badger*. In addition to the provision of refreshment for the local population and the visitors who came to enjoy the rural surroundings, the inn provided a room which was used as a school-room. Children ceased to attend at the inn when the chapel-cum-schoolhouse was built at Addington Hills. It is likely that the first people to settle in this small valley were squatters, and for many years the district was ex-parochial, i.e., it was not part of either Croydon, Addington, or Shirley. On the tithe map of Addington (*c.* 1842), however, the area is shown as definitely within the parish of Addington.

The Lamb was another inn nestling in the shadows of Addington Hills. It stood alone in a valley near Coombe Lane between the site of a reservoir and the road which links Coombe Lane with Shirley Hills Road—a small thatched building with a reputation of being the haunt of smugglers. After they had made a long night ride from the coast, with kegs of Hollands or brandy carried before and behind their saddles, they were said to have rested in this well-hidden inn until it was safe to resume their journey towards London. Local legends tell of sundry clashes with 'the excise men' on these 'ancient Surrey Hills'. The valley in which the inn stood was known in Addington as Breakneck Hollow, a name that is supposed to have derived from the fact that a visitor to the inn, having drunk copiously of the host's liquor, tried to ride his horse straight up the steepest part of the valley side. The horse shied, the rider fell heavily, and was killed. The earliest known tenants of the inn were members of a family named Norwood, sometimes written Norhood or Norrod, in the 17th century. The last landlord of *The Lamb* was Richard Gunner, and he moved from that side of Addington Hills to Badger's Hole round about 1830, when the inn was demolished.

The only other district of Addington to have been called a hamlet was Bandy Mount or Boundary Mount. It really only consisted of a few houses on the Ballards estate, lying along Coombe Lane between the two entrances to the present Ballards school. The name could have come from the roadway itself, which forms the boundary between Addington Hills and the Ballards Plantation. It is said to have been the site of many a prize-fight in the days when boxing gloves were unknown, and contests lasted until one of the fighters was unable to continue. It is just possible that the alternative name of Bandy Mount may be connected with the game of cricket. It will be remembered that the curved bat used in the 18th century was also called a 'bandy', and records exist telling of matches played on Addington Hills. As the only suitably flat playing area on the hills is bounded on the Coombe Lane side by Bandy Mount a connection between that area and the cricketers of Addington is not impossible.

Chapter Seven

TOWARDS THE FUTURE

ACCORDING TO THE DOMESDAY RECORD there were in 1086 two manors in this part of the county of Surrey, each under the control of a lord of the manor. In addition to the two lords there were 13 'villeins' and 13 'cottars', making a total of 28 individuals. Canon Benham[1] is reputed to have suggested that each of these persons would have been the head of a family, and that the average size of such a unit would have been five people. It was reasoned that on the basis of the figures given, the population of Addington would have amounted to 140 persons. It is interesting to note that when the first National Census was taken in 1801 there were 178 inhabitants of Addington. An increase of only 38 people over a period of 700 years represents an average rate of growth of five persons every 100 years. That seems too low a figure to be true, and if it is accepted as a mean then some of the years between 1086 and 1801 must have shown considerably higher numbers.

John Aubrey[2] wrote of 'local inhabitants who talk of tradition . . . that Addington was anciently far bigger than now, not only to vie with any in these parts, but for Inns or Publick Houses to infinitely surpass them'. There are some people who refuse to dismiss every legendary story as nonsense, and they may feel that Aubrey's account of the thoughts of Addington's 17th- or 18th-century inhabitants support a belief that some evidence of such a larger Addington may still lie buried beneath its soil. Perhaps, before the last few fields of this ancient place disappear for ever under the ever-spreading suburban sprawl of Greater London, one final effort may be made to settle the matter one way or the other.

The last individual to claim lordship of the manor of Addington was F. A. English, Esq.,[3] and when he died in 1909 the already diminished status of Addington as an ancient manorial estate was lost for ever. The provision of agricultural and dairy products, however, went on as before, and the farmers of Addington continued to send their produce to the markets and shops of Croydon and neighbouring districts. The continuance of the rustic peace of Addington village seemed to be secure. Yet an event occurred, which although in no way directly connected with the history of Addington, gave the old village a gentle push into the young 20th century.

It was in 1909 that the French aviator, Louis Bleriot, made his famous flight across the English Channel from Calais to Dover. His achievement, following the successes of the Wright brothers in America, stimulated similar interest in Britain. As a result two pioneer airmen from London, the brothers Sydney and Arthur Zippi, designed and built a monoplane and brought it to Addington to test its capabilities. They came to a field off Lodge Lane, just below the present Fieldway estate, and made several attempts to get it into the air, but without success. That was in 1910, but they evidently succeeded elsewhere at a later date, for their machine was subsequently described as 'the first practical monoplane'. Sydney Zippi later became a distinguished member of the Royal Flying Corps, serving as a pilot in the First World War.

Soon after war began in 1914, a searchlight was erected in Addington to scan the night skies for any airship or aeroplane the enemy might send against us. This searchlight stood in Church Meadow against the boundary of the field in which the Zippi brothers had experimented with their monoplane a few years earlier. When the war was over Grahame White—another pioneer of powered flight— made a forced landing in another field off Lodge Lane. That field was nearer to New Addington and is now crossed by the modern roads Walton Green and Dunsfold Way. After repairs were completed Grahame White flew off to the newly-opened Croydon airport.

Addington's links with aviation did not end with these incidents. In 1930 application was made by an air transport company for the use of a field at Addington as a private aerodrome. Croydon Corporation objected on environmental grounds, but were overruled by the Ministry of Health. The Air Ministry sanctioned the use of the field in the spring of 1932. The area involved lay between Featherbed Lane and Lodge Lane, and extended from St Edward's church to Fairchilds school, at New Addington. Milne Park playing field is all that is now left of the aerodrome. When the airfield was in operation it was used as a school for the training of pilots employed by the transport firm. Other small aircraft also used the field, some by solo fliers, some carrying one or two passengers. An air pageant was held in 1933, when aerobatics, parachute jumping, and wing walking were some of the attractions. The field was not used as an aerodrome during the 1939–45 War, and the property and buildings that belonged to the air transport company were removed to Gatwick in 1944.

The great need during both wars was to grow more food, and between 1914 and 1918 some extra houses were built in Addington to house the workers needed to increase the production of the local farms. The 'Cocestre' cottages in the Village Road were among the new houses of the period. Addington Palace, once the home of archbishops, became a hospital for members of the armed forces. Wars, of course, have to come to an end, and men return to their homes and take up the pursuits of peace once more. For many of them this was impossible, and new employment had to be found for them. A move to assist in this resettlement of ex-service men was made in Addington by the Surrey Garden Village Trust, Ltd., who put forward plans for the purchase of 533 acres of Addington farmland on which a Garden Village would be built. There were to be a number of smallholdings, varying in size from half an acre upwards. Houses would be built, with access roads and a recreation ground. All the ground between Lodge Lane and the Addington–Selsdon border was included, but during negotiations the eastern half was withdrawn and only the land west of Featherbed Lane was bought. This was divided into about 100 plots and by 1928 they had all been sold and houses were standing on most of them. The smallholders produced pigs and poultry, fruit and flowers, and vegetables of all kinds. They formed their own co-operative marketing unit with a building at the end of Featherbed Lane, which is now a restaurant. The venture met with varying degrees of success and survived until the 1960s when the whole area was bought by a development company. It is now covered with houses, and is called Forestdale.

During the development of the smallholdings new houses began to appear on part of Addington Lodge Farm at what is now New Addington. These were erected by a body called The First National Housing Trust and were to be let at 'reasonable rents'. They were built on land between the present *Addington Hotel* and Salcot Crescent. Gascoigne Road, Wolsey Crescent, and Parkway formed the boundaries of the first section to be completed. It was intended to extend the estate southwards for a considerable distance, but for various reasons (including the remoteness of the area, its exposed position, and the lack of transport facilities to and from Croydon) the rate of building slowed a little. The development of the first part was completed by about 1935, and by that time there were shops providing a reasonable service to the community, and transport had improved to some extent.

Nearer to the village of Addington, close to Featherbed Lane and Gravel Hill, another housing estate was being developed. In 1936–7, however, an outbreak of typhoid fever occurred in Croydon, and the Croydon Corporation's well in Featherbed Lane was suspected of being the source of the epidemic. Despite the fact that water from that particular well was not being distributed to any of the houses in Addington, the association of the district with the disease effectively discouraged would-be house buyers from coming to Addington at that time. The international situation was not encouraging either. The clouds of war were already gathering, and when the conflict began in 1939 all building stopped.

During the war, Addington did not escape the attentions of the enemy. Indeed, the first bombs to be dropped near Croydon fell in Addington village in June 1940. The missiles were small and did little serious damage, except to the field of strawberries in which they fell. Later on, local residents in all parts of Addington watched waves of enemy bombers pass over Addington on their way to London. Fighter planes from the aerodromes at Biggin Hill, Croydon, and Kenley engaged the attacking force, and many an aerial battle was fought in the skies above the fields of Addington. Some bombs, perhaps intended for the airfields just mentioned, fell near the New Addington Shopping Centre and some in nearby streets, resulting in casualties among the residents and damage to properties. In the closing years of the war the enemy were using flying bombs and rockets, and at least three of the former and one of the latter made their mark on Addington soil. To these must be added incendiary bombs by the thousand. It was fortunate that there was, in those disturbing times, plenty of open space. There is no doubt that a similar attack in the future would have much more serious results.

Addington parish had been merged with what was then the County Borough of Croydon in 1927, and a year later that authority bought all of the farmlands south of the Village Road. The territory was then leased back to the farmers until such time as it would be needed for the erection of council houses under building plans yet to be devised. That time came after the last war, when many Croydon families had been rendered homeless as a result of enemy action. Prefabricated housing units were erected on part of Castle Hill Farm (off Lodge Lane), and on Monks Hill (part of Heathfield Farm), off Selsdon Park Road. More houses of the same type were put on the few remaining fields on the Spring Park Estate. When these were finished and occupied, the provision of more permanent dwellings began in earnest. As the post-war years passed by, more and more houses and flats, schools and shops were built until the operations ended with the completion of the Fieldway Estate.

Simultaneously with the building of all these houses a factory estate was developed on the eastern boundary of New Addington. Many trades and services were represented, among them both light and heavy engineering, cabinet-making, food-processing, and the new science of electronics. Instruments from the latter source were incorporated in the American spacecraft that carried men a quarter of a million miles to the surface of the moon. In marked contrast to the marvels of modern science, there are, behind the factories, the remains of a Roman road along which marched men more interested in conquering Britain than in exploring space.

NOTES

Chapter One

1. Blount, T., *Ancient Tenures* (1679), hereafter Blount.
2. Mills, W. H., *Proceedings of the Croydon Natural History and Scientific Society* (hereafter *C.N.H.S.S.*) (1916), vol. 8, iv, pp. 161–173.
3. Mills, W. H., and Roberts, N., *C.N.H.S.S.* (1917-1918).
4. Johnson, W., and Wright, W., *Neolithic Man in North East Surrey* (1903).
5. Mills, W. H., *C.N.H.S.S.* (1916), vol. 8, iv, p. 164.
6. Haigh, D. H., *The Conquest of Britain by the Saxons* (1861).
7. Dugdale, Thomas, *England and Wales Delineated* (1854-60), hereafter Dugdale.
8. Aubrey, John, *The Natural History and Antiquities of Surrey* (1718-19), hereafter Aubrey.

Chapter Two

1. Godsal, P. T., *The Storming of London and the Thames Valley Campaign: a Military Study of the Conquest of Britain by the Angles* (1908).
2. Major, A. F., 'The Presidential Address', *C.N.H.S.S.* (1920-1), vol. 12.
3. Walford, Edward, *Greater London* (1885), hereafter Walford, vol. 2, pp. 130 *et seq.*
4. Public Record Office, Wills of the Prerogative Court of Canterbury, hereafter P.C.C., Fenner 24, will of Sir Olliphe Leigh.

Chapter Three

1. Manning, Owen, and Bray, W., *The history and antiquities of the county of Surrey* (1804-14), hereafter Manning Bray, vol. 3, p. 363.
2. Turner, Frederick, 'Addington: Charters of St Mary Overie', *Surrey Archaeological Collections*, vol. 31, p. 129 (hereafter Turner).
3. *Victoria County History of Surrey*, vol. 3, p. 436.
4. *Victoria County History of Sussex*, vol. 1, p. 378.
5. Salzman, L. F., 'The family of Chesney', *Sussex Archaeological Collections*, vol. 1, p. 15.
6. Mills, W. H., 'A dictionary of parochial biography' (typescript, Mills Collection in Croydon Reference Library, hereafter Mills Collection).
7. Malden, H. E., *A History of Surrey* (1877), p. 5.
8. Turner, p. 129.
9. Page, William, *London: its origins and early development* (1923).
10. 'Thegn' is a term comparable with 'lord of the manor'.
11. 'The Cartulary of St John's, Colchester', *Roxburgh Club*, vol. 1, p. 28.
12. *Victoria County History of Hertfordshire*, vol. 1, pp. 285, 342; vol. 3, pp. 138, 154, 159; vol. 4, p. 291.
13. *Transactions of the London and Middlesex Archaeological Society*, vol. 42.
14. *Pipe Roll Society*, vol. 8, p. 124; vol. 10, p. 154.

15. This abbey was founded by Ailwin Childe. *See* Besant, W., *South London*, p. 52.

16. Lysons, Daniel, *Environs of London* (1811 edition), hereafter Lysons, pp. 1-6.

17. Salzman, L. F., 'The family of Aguillon' (hereafter Salzman), *Sussex Archaeological Collections*, vol. 79, p. 45 *et seq.*

18. Turner, pp. 129-133.

19. *Rot de Obl. et Fines*, p. 489.

20. Salzman, pp. 45-60.

21. *Ibid.*, p. 56.

22. Curia Regis Rolls, vol. 7, p. 71; Salzman.

23. Curia Regis Rolls, 77, m. 12.

24. Salzman, pp. 45-60.

25. Britton, J., and Brayley, E. W., *Beauties of England and Wales* (1813), hereafter Britton and Brayley, vol. 14.

26. Red Book of Exchequer, 754.

27. Brayley, E. Wedlake, *A Topographical History of Surrey* (1850), hereafter Brayley, vol. 14, pp. 24-31.

28. Manning and Bray, vol. 2, p. 557 *et seq.*

29. Cal. Chart R. 1226-57, p. 329.

30. Salzman, p. 45 *et seq.*

31. Curia Regis Rolls, 154, m. 243.

32. Cal. Pat. 495.

33. Stapleton, p. 17 (hereafter Stapleton).

34. Exc. & Rot. Fin., ii, 590.

35. Stapleton, p. 28.

36. *Sussex Record Society*, vol. 7, no. 742.

37. Stapleton, p. 32.

38. *Sussex Record Society*, vol. 7, nos. 643, 655, 748, 834.

39. Pat. 54, Hen. III, m. 26.

40. *C.N.H.S.S.*, vol. 8, iv, p. 171.

41. Stapleton, *op. cit.*

42. Calendar of Wills in the Court of Hastings.

43. *Dictionary of National Biography.*

44. de Walden, Lord Howard, *Some Feudal Lords and their Seals*, 1904 (hereafter de Walden).

45. Britton and Brayley, p. 417.

46. Cokayne, G. C. (ed.), *The Complete Peerage* (hereafter Cokayne) (1910), p. 417.

47. Inquisition Post Mortem, 14 Oct., Edward I (1304).

48. *Calendar of Patent Rolls 1317-1321*, p. 135; Feet of Fines DN Co. 11 and 12, Ed. II, no. 168; *Victoria County History of Surrey*, vol. 4, p. 164 *et seq.*

49. de Walden.

50. Cokayne.

51. de Walden.

52. Cokayne.

53. Jones, W., *Crowns and Coronations*, p. 115; and Close Rolls 1, Richard II (Coronation Claims), m. 44.

54. *Victoria County History of Surrey*, vol. 4, p. 165.

55. Inquisition Post Mortem, 2, Rich. II, no. 104 may be relevant.

56. Cokayne.

57. *See* Shakespeare, William, *Henry IV, part 2.*

58. Leveson-Gower, G., 'Notices of the Leigh family of Addington' (typescript in the Mills Collection, hereafter Leveson-Gower); Deed of 25 Nov, Hen. VI (Lambeth Palace Library).

59. Leveson-Gower.

60. Ped. Fin. 45, Edw. III, no. 93.

61. Claus of Rich. II, no. 24.
62. This deed is in Lambeth Palace Library.
63. Deed 6 Mar. 1453, 32, Hen. VI (Lambeth Palace Library).
64. Hasted, Edward, *The history and topographical survey of the County of Kent* (1778-99), vol. 8, p. 40, refers to an ancient manor of 'Bottsham' but does not mention any person of that name.
65. Fox, Tom. III, fo. 616.
66. Lysons, vol. 1, p. 9.
67. Manning and Bray, vol. 2, p. 559
68. Leveson-Gower.
69. 'Pedigree of Founder's Kin' (Lambeth Palace Library MSS.).
70. Folio 201; Reg. F.; Canterbury; inquisition Post Mortem, 19 Apr., Henry VII, no. 7.
71. Charter of John Leigh, 10 June, 3 Rich III. (In Lambeth Palace Library).
72. Manning and Bray; Brayley, vol. 4, pp. 24-31.
73. 25 June, 36 Henry VIII, quoted in Turner, pp. 129-133.
74. Deed 20 Mar., 18 Elizabeth I, between Nicholas Leigh, John and Joan Leigh (*see* Addington Deeds, Lambeth Palace Library).
75. Principal Reg. Probate Court, Archdeaconry of Surrey.
76. Manning and Bray, vol. 2, p. 557; vol. 3, p. 365.
77. Brayley, vol. 14, pp. 24-31.
78. Leveson-Gower.
79. Camden, William, *Britannia* (1586: Gough's translation).
80. The story of these excursions was published in the *Naval Chronicle* in the 19th century.
81. Leveson-Gower.
82. Paget, C. G., *Croydon Homes of the Past* (1937).
83. *Calendar of State Papers*, 1603-1630.
84. P.C.C., Fenner 24, Will of Sir Olliphe Leigh.
85. *Calendar of State Papers Domestic, 1631-1633*, pp. 82 and 189; and *ibid., 1636-1637*, pp. 242-404, cited in Leveson-Gower.
86. *Croydon in the Past*, published by the *Croydon Advertiser*, December 1883.
87. Leveson-Gower.
88. P.C.C., Rivers 54, Will of Sir Francis Leigh.
89. The name 'Wolley' was his maternal grandmother's maiden name.
90. Blount.
91. Leveson-Gower.
92. Plans and a 'view' were published in *Vitruvius Britannicus*, 1771.
93. Lysons.
94. Brayley, vol. 4, pp. 24-31.
95. Walford, vol. 2, pp. 130 *et seq.*
96. Mills, W. H., 'Queen Emma's Seat', in Mills Collection, Folder 5.

Chapter Four

1. Salzman.
2. *Victoria County History of Surrey*, vol. 2, p. 51; Pat. 54, Hen. III, m. 26.
3. Aubrey.
4. Benham, Revd. W., 'Gleanings of Addington's History' (1877), Mills Collection, hereafter Benham.
5. *Croydon Advertiser*, 20 July 1973.
6. i.e., Warlingham.
7. Mills Collection.
8. *Ibid.*

9. *Victoria County History of Surrey*, vol. 4, p. 493.
10. Anderson, J. C., *Croydon Inclosures*, part 1 (1801).
11. *Victoria County History of Surrey*, vol. 4, p. 164.
12. *C.N.H.S.S.* (1971), vol. 14, ix, p. 208.
13. *The Second Symposium of the Archaeology of Croydon*, published by the Croydon Natural History and Scientific Society (1970-2).
14. Benham.
15. 'Lombard, Peter' [pseudonym], 'Addington', *McMillan's Magazine* (1883).
16. Mills Collection.
17. *Surrey Magazine*, 1903, p. 238.
18. Lysons, pp. 1-6.
19. *C.N.H.S.S.* (1973), p. 441.
20. Benham, W., 'Addington Manor', MS. in Mills Collection.
21. A John Leigh bought Addington Manor from William Uvedale, 1447 (*see* Chapter Three).
22. Claus of Rich. II, no. 24.
23. *C.N.H.S.S.*, vol. 8, iv, p. 170.
24. *Bibliolithica Topographica Britannica*, vol. 2, appendix to *History of Croydon*, no. 46, p. 184.
25. *The Gentleman's Magazine*, vol. 69, p. 833-844.
26. Camden, William, *Britannia* (1586).

Chapter Five

1. Charters of Richard, Bishop of Winchester, 3 May 1174-22 Dec. 1185.
2. Mainwaring, Philip, *Surrey Archaeological Collections*, vol. 14, p. 114.
3. Folio 201, Reg. F; Canterbury Inquisitions Post Mortem, 19 Apr., Henry VIII, no. 7.
4. The 'faculty' authorising the reredos lists 'Augustine' in place of 'Theodore'.
5. Benham.
6. Leveson-Gower.
7. The old organ was moved here *c.* 1875 and rebuilt and enlarged in 1932.
8. *Surrey Archaeological Collections*, vol. 4, pp. 62-3.
9. Aubrey.
10. Mills Collection.
11. *Surrey Archaeological Collections*, vol. 4, p. 62.
12. Mills Collection.

Chapter Six

1. Charter, 2 Edward II.
2. *Victoria County History of Surrey*, vol. 4, p. 493.
3. P.C.C., Fenner 24.
4. *The Statesman*, 9 May 1815; *Bell's Sunday Despatch*, 4 May 1817.
5. In metric terms, 25p and 12½p respectively.

Chapter Seven

1. He was vicar 1867-73, and wrote 'Gleanings of Addington's History' about 1877. Under the pen-name 'Peter Lombard' wrote 'Addington', published in *Macmillan Magazine*, 1883.
2. Aubrey.
3. *See* Chapter Three, part 8.

APPENDIX

A Schedule suggesting a possible division of Addington lands, named as Ed*d*intone and E*d*intone in the Domesday Record *c.* 1086

The names of the holders are given in the Survey as follows:

Albert held Ed*d*intone

Tezelin held E*d*intone

The approximate acreage of the Parish of Addington was 3,530. Albert had 7½ hides; Tezelin had 8½ hides. (A hide is assumed to equal 120 acres).

Area	Albert	Tezelin	Mearc	Total
	acres	acres	acres	acres
Monks Orchard	—	—	250	250
Spring Park	—	—	450	450
Addington Park	—	450	—	450
Heathfield	—	250	—	250
Ballards	—	—	290	290
Upper and Lower Farms	—	320	—	320
Castle Hill Farm	250	—	—	250
Addington Lodge Farm	650	—	—	650
Addington Hills, and Forestdale, Frith Wood, Bears Wood, Lady Grove, Frylands Wood, and the woods on the eastern boundary	—	—	620	620
Totals	900	1,020	1,610	3,530

The total of 3,530 acres maintains the Domesday proportions between the two manors, and the dividing line follows long established field boundaries.

There seems to be no doubt that the more important of the two manors was that of Tezelin. The documentation of its long history is proof of that. It is unfortunate that no comparable records of Albert's manor is available in order that a full account of both territories might be presented.

INDEX

Compiled by Angela Tredell

LIST OF SUBSCRIBERS

Hazel C. Ainsworth
Applegarth Junior School
Reginald G. E. Armfield
Martyn Arnold, Esq.
Mrs. Maureen Atkinson
Peter Baker
Raymond P. Baker
T. M. Baker
Mr. and Mrs. M. Ball
Kenneth John Barrance
David G. Bate
Caryl Beach
Mrs. M. M. Bennett
Mrs. B. L. P. Blanchette
Mrs. Dora Bourne
Miss Hazel Bourne
Miss Heather Bourne
J. H. Bowers
D. H. Bray
Maurice Bristow
Mrs. J. A. Brown
H. G. A. Browne
M. Burnett
Paddy Burnham
Barry O'Byrne
Janet Carlyle
Castle Hill Junior School
Christine Callender (née Bramley)
Frank and Jill Cantelo
Jeanette M. H. Carter
Stanley Cheetham
Matthew James Cheval
Audrey Clark
Robert and Laurel Clinton
Angela Cocks
Carolyn Cocks
Christopher Cocks
Jack and Mavis Cocks
Penelope Cocks
Mrs. Audrey Coe
Mrs. Coles
Marianne Collins
Christopher John Michael Cooney
M. L. Corless
Dr. R. C. W. Cox
Mrs. Patricia Crane
Peter C. Crane
Lorraine Creech

Croydon Natural History and Scientific Society
Croydon R. E. Resource Centre
Dr. and Mrs. Lionel Dakers
S. Dansey
Mrs. Anne Davenport
Rita Davey
Mark Davison
Richard O. C. Dayus
Mervyn Dell
Mr. Robert C. Dodson
Alfred Doherty
Brian and Chris Dooley
Mr. James A. Druce
Miss E. M. Dull
Peter Duncan
Mr. J. N. Edmonds
Donald J. Edwards
Mrs. Vera Eisner
George Sidney Ellis
Mrs. Linda J. Evans
Leonard James Failes
D. K. Fairbairn
Fairchildes High School
Roger and Kathleen FitzPatrick
Robert W. Fleckney
Forestdale Primary School
D. L. Forsdick
Robert Fox
Mr. H. Frankland
H. Franklin
J. A. Freegard
Charles French
Edith L. Frewin
Eileen Frost
John Furlonger
Mrs. A. S. Galer
John B. Gent
Gilbert Scott Junior School
Mr. and Mrs. R. C. Gill
Mrs. J. Gillett
Sarah Jane Glanville
E. C. H. Godfrey
H. G. Gooding, B.Sc. (Econ.)
M. S. Goldsmith
Steven Gray
John and Mary Graystone
P. W. Green

Nick and Madge Gregory
R. C. and J. M. Haite
Emma C. Halpin
Doreen Harris
Frederick E. Hayman
Barbara and Philip Heseltine
Catherine A. Hickmott
Mr. N. J. Higerty
Mr. and Mrs. C. Hobbs
Doris C. H. Hobbs
Dr. Doreen Hobson
D. R. and C. E. Hodges
N. V. Holloway, Esq.
June Holmes
Mrs. F. Hope
Mrs. Florence Hope
Jessie M. Hudleston
John and Marian Hughes
Muriel Huitson
P. J. Hulyer
Grace A. Hunt
Mrs. Trudy Hunt
Frank Jefkins
K. N. Johnceline
Miss J. N. Lambert
Elfreda Johnson
Peter Johnstone
Anita Jones
Reginald Newell Jones
Olga Kennedy
Mrs. Daphne King
David J. King
Graham King
Mr. and Mrs. H. C. King
Michael P. King
Karin and Christian Kuepers
P. Latham
Alan Lindsay
Mrs. J. E. McCubbins
John McDermott
Maureen McFie
David McGrath
Mrs. Margaret McQueen
David B. Mahoney
Tod Marshall
Mrs. W. R. Martin
The Masters family
A. V. Mascull

List of Subscribers—*continued*

John D. Matthews
Bill Mitchell
Margaret D. Mitchell
Mr. C. J. Monk
Monks Hill High School
Jack Moon
The Reverend Christopher Morgan-
    Jones
Clifford M. Mould
Narindar Nath, F.D.S., Dip. D.R.Th.
    R.C.S.
Draruna Nath, M.R.C.O.C.
New Addington Good Samaritans
P. E. Newnham
John Newman High School, Geog.
    Dept.
Mrs. J. Nicol
Mrs. Doreen Normandale
Mrs. M. Norton
Brian R. Orbell
Daniel Leslie Osborne
Hon. Ald. William Norman Peet
A. J. Pelling
D. R. Penfold
B. Philibert
M. A. A. Pole
L. Preston
Gwen Prosser
Doris E. Pullen
F. H. Pyefinch

Mr. and Mrs. Radley
Hon. Ald. Brian H. Rawling, J.P.
Eleanor Redshaw
Jacquelin Reed
Jean Frances Reeves
Gary Revel-Chion, B.Sc. (Econ.)
William Frosdick Rhodes
Douglas R. Richmond
Mr. R. Rogowski
Helga Lily Roos
Marjorie M. Rorke
Royal Russell School Library
D. H. and D. D. Sander
Alex Sanson, C.B.E.
Anthony Sapwell
Sir Donald Sargent, K.B.E., C.B.,
    F.P.M.I.
Mark and Gary Saunders
Gordon Savage
Jennifer M. S. Scherr
Selsdon Primary School
Jane Shaw
Edwin Short
M. E. Short
Douglas A. Simmons
Margaret Simpson
The Slater family
Colin S. Smith
Roy J. Smith
Barbara Softly

Paul W. Sowan
David Staplin
G. J. Stebbing
R. G. Stevens
H. R. E. Surridge
Harry Jack Pride Taylor
Michael A. Taylor
Lilian Thornhill
M. Tipton
Pat and Roy Topp
John G. Trimmer
Philip A. Truett
Beverley A. Tugwell
T. Voltz
B. Wakeling
Dr. Wendy Wallace
J. L. Warner
Peter John Warren
Vincent Waterhouse
Edith Maud White
William John Whybrow
H. S. Wightman
Henry C. Wilks
D. F. Willey
J. Alan Willey
John M. Williams
B. E. Winscom
W. Jeffrey Wonham
David J. York
James A. Young